WALKING COUNTRY

COAST TO COAST
WALK

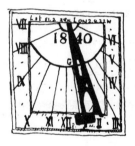

Paul Hannon

HILLSIDE

HILLSIDE
PUBLICATIONS
12 Broadlands
Shann Park
Keighley
West Yorkshire
BD20 6HX

First published 1992
Revised 1997
7th (updated) impression 2004

© Paul Hannon 1992, 2004

ISBN 1 870141 55 5

TO
The Silver Jubilee Coast to Coasters,
Especially my good companion Pete

The maps in this book are based upon
1900-1930 Ordnance Survey 1:10,560 maps
The route in this book is based on the route described in
'A Coast to Coast Walk' by A. Wainwright,
Michael Joseph 1992 (originally Westmorland Gazette 1972)

WALKING COUNTRY

COAST TO COAST WALK

Paul Hannon

HILLSIDE GUIDES - ACROSS THE NORTH & BEYOND

The Uplands of Britain
- **THE HIGH PEAKS OF ENGLAND & WALES**
- **YORKSHIRE DALES, MOORS & FELLS**

Long Distance Walks
- **COAST TO COAST WALK**   • **DALES WAY**   • **CLEVELAND WAY**
- **WESTMORLAND WAY**   • **FURNESS WAY**
- **BRONTE WAY**   • **PENDLE WAY**   • **NIDDERDALE WAY**
- **LADY ANNE'S WAY**   • **TRANS-PENNINE WAY**   • **CALDERDALE WAY**

Hillwalking - Lake District
- **LAKELAND FELLS - SOUTH**   • **LAKELAND FELLS - EAST**
- **LAKELAND FELLS - NORTH**   • **LAKELAND FELLS - WEST**

Circular Walks - Peak District
- **NORTHERN PEAK**   • **EASTERN PEAK**   • **CENTRAL PEAK**
- **SOUTHERN PEAK**   • **WESTERN PEAK**

Circular Walks - Yorkshire Dales
- **HOWGILL FELLS**   • **THREE PEAKS**   • **MALHAMDALE**
- **WHARFEDALE**   • **NIDDERDALE**   • **WENSLEYDALE**   • **SWALEDALE**

Circular Walks - North York Moors
- **WESTERN MOORS**   • **SOUTHERN MOORS**

Circular Walks - South Pennines
- **BRONTE COUNTRY**   • **ILKLEY MOOR**
- **CALDERDALE**   • **SOUTHERN PENNINES**

Circular Walks - Lancashire
- **BOWLAND**   • **PENDLE & THE RIBBLE**   • **WEST PENNINE MOORS**

Circular Walks - North Pennines
- **TEESDALE**   • **EDEN VALLEY**   • **ALSTON & ALLENDALE**

WayMaster Guides - Short Scenic Walks
- **ESKDALE, North York Moors**   • **WHARFEDALE, Yorkshire Dales**
- **AMBLESIDE & LANGDALE, Lake District**

City Theme Walks   • **YORK WALKS**

Pocket Biking Guides
- **WHARFEDALE BIKING GUIDE**
- **AIRE VALLEY BIKING GUIDE**   • **CALDERDALE BIKING GUIDE**

WayMaster Visitor Guides • **YORKSHIRE DALES**

Send for a detailed current catalogue and pricelist,
and also visit *www.hillsidepublications.co.uk*

CONTENTS

Great Gable from Innominate Tarn, Haystacks

St Bees Head

Robin Hood's Bay

INTRODUCTION

Coast to Coast - the very name is inspiring, from clifftop to clifftop across our small but perfectly formed land, magnificent strides through some of the grandest scenery in the North. The mountains of Lakeland, the Pennine uplands, glorious Swaledale, the Cleveland Hills, and Eskdale and the North York Moors, so much magic in so little space! Little wonder that walkers relish its clarion call, and enthuse ever afterwards over its finest moments.

As originator of the Coast to Coast Walk in the early 1970s, the late A. Wainwright was a hallowed name to tens of thousands of hillwalkers through his previous guidebooks. Subsequently, for better or worse, the media transformed him into a household name, and the end result is that few people have not now heard of the Coast to Coast Walk. Having devised the entire route himself through his personal cross-section of the North's best walking country, it may be regarded as his finest hour, and as such is just that little bit special.

As a long-standing admirer of the walk's creator it gave me particular satisfaction to produce, in 1992, the first new guide to the route since Wainwright's original masterpiece. At that time the original work had not kept pace with the countless changes of two decades: the route's thousands of walkers badly needed to be re-directed onto the right paths and supplied with up to date supporting information. This pleasurable task was savoured as a personal tribute to Wainwright, a far more practical memorial than a cairn or a re-named tarn. In his glory days Wainwright was never less than a perfectionist, and if this guide falls short of his exacting standards, he would surely have been happy to see his followers on the right track.

Compiled in 1997, this new edition adds the changes of the last five years to those of the previous two decades, from inevitable ones such as hedges being ripped up, and new stiles and waymarking to those brought about by path diversions, creations, or to accommodate the wishes of landowners. Various suggestions for local alternatives on rights of way are included, though the guide adheres to the original route where it remains in common use. On a couple of occasions I have introduced the walk to logically sited public footpaths to avoid entirely unnecessary and potentially dangerous road walking.

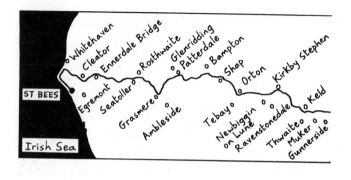

Old chapel, Keld

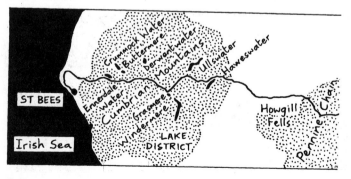

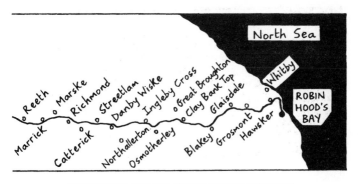

Hasty Bank across Clay Bank Top

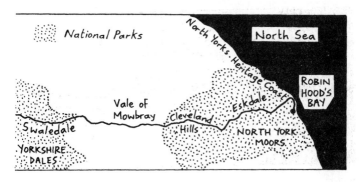

PLANNING THE WALK

The Coast to Coast Walk runs from St Bees on the Cumbrian coast to Robin Hood's Bay on the Yorkshire coast, a distance of some 190 miles. Within these pages the walk has been divided into 12 different stages for practical purposes, but as the sketch maps and mileages are continuous, this will have little effect on each individual's chosen route. Most people will be aiming to complete the walk within a two week period, which would normally allow 14 overnights.

Thanks to the growing number of establishments catering for Coast to Coast walkers (particularly welcome in areas outside the National Parks) any number of permutations can be devised to suit one's needs. Unless planning to come out of season it is vital to book in advance to ensure a bed at the end of each day. Campers are well catered for, on the whole, and are more likely to get by on a casual day to day basis. Page 11 has some suggestions for varying the overnight stops.

A welcome addition to the range of accommodation options is the proliferation of bunkhouses and camping barns. Currently these can be found at or near Sandwith, Rosthwaite, Shap, Newbiggin on Lune, Ravenstonedale, Low Row, Applegarth (Richmond), Brompton on Swale, Lovesome Hill (Oaktree Hill), Farndale Head and Westerdale. Those from Low Row eastwards can be booked through the YHA Northern Region.

The unexpected popularity of the walk has led to a cottage industry in the provision of accommodation lists, which sell in their own right as little booklets. They are of great value as the walk passes through many different districts, and collating the necessary information might otherwise be a complicated affair. These booklets can be found in some shops, or obtained from the sources listed on page 16 (ring for availability and prices). The North York Moors Adventure Centre can also provide badges, T-shirts and completion certificates.

The Youth Hostels Association operates an accommodation booking bureau through which the entire walk can be booked in one fell swoop, selecting your own overnights along the way. Many of these are, quite obviously, at youth hostels, but where not available an appropriate B + B will be booked. For a small service charge this saves the hassle of dealing with a dozen or more different places. (See YHA Northern Region, again, for an information package).

In practise the 12 main sections form a reasonable basis, but some useful variations are listed below (route alternatives within each section are included in their respective introduction).

◆ If not leaving St Bees first thing, re-adjust the first two days by halting before Ennerdale: it still shouldn't be too far to Rosthwaite on the second day.

◆ Break up Stage 3 with an overnight at Grasmere, permitting a more adventurous walk the second day, or simply time to sample Grasmere.

◆ Split Stages 4 and 5 into three days by breaking at or around Bampton and Orton, instead of Shap.

◆ Break up Stage 5 in the Newbiggin on Lune area in place of Kirkby Stephen - this splits Stages 5 and 6 more evenly.

◆ Anyone wishing to save a day could merge Stages 6, 7 and 8 into two, if taking the valley route rather than the moors route through Swaledale, in which case several villages offer a break.

◆ As Stage 8 is such a short one, continue it to Catterick Bridge. If wishing to sample Richmond, return to it by bus and catch it back out to Catterick Bridge in the morning. Alternatively, simply break up Stage 9 at any of several locations, allowing a later departure from Richmond.

◆ Extend the final three days into four by substituting Glaisdale with Blakey and Grosmont. This is a little uneven though, as Clay Bank Top to Blakey will probably be deemed too short, and in any case the miles do continue very easily to Glaisdale. However, if descending into Farndale for the 'Blakey' over-night, then it might seem enough of a day. If keeping to three days from Ingleby Cross to the sea, an alternative is simply to replace Clay Bank Top with Blakey (a longer day), and Glaisdale with Grosmont (two shorter days).

◆ If aiming for a same day getaway from Robin Hood's Bay, break the final stage at Hawsker for a lunchtime finish at Robin Hood's Bay.

The popularity of the walk has also brought about very useful transport services created specifically for Coast to Coast walkers. Two firms specialise in carrying either weary people or simply groaning rucksacks to and from locations along the entire length of the route. Through them you can enjoy long days with a light daypack; 'skip' a day if needing a rest; or enjoy the most direct return to your car or starting point. Secure car parking facilities are also available.

The Coast to Coast Packhorse is based plum on the walk, almost midway at Kirkby Stephen, and can arrange a full package holiday. Its bus service is also a scheduled public transport facility, which claims to be the longest rural passenger bus service in England! The White Knight is operated by In Step, and offers similar services with various permutations. Both have been established for some years, and an enquiry will elicit their current arrangements (see page 16).

Access to the start and finish of the route is not too difficult. St Bees is on the Cumbrian coast railway line, and its station connects with Carlisle (north) and Barrow, for Lancaster (south). Robin Hood's Bay long since lost its station, but is served by the Whitby-Scarborough bus which links with railway stations in both towns. Certainly if heading south then the longer bus ride to Scarborough will find one with a better service to the main line at York.

A very practical problem over the years has been the dearth of 'hole in the wall' cash dispensers along the route, leading to potentially embarrassing situations! Things have now improved and currently both Kirkby Stephen and Richmond offer this facility. The very few banks that can be found are rarely open at suitable times for Coast to Coast walkers, though post offices are more likely to prove of value. A cheque book should therefore supplement a supply of ready cash.

Finally, bear in mind that coffee table books and television portray only the glamorous side of a long-distance walk, giving little mention of blood, sweat and tears. Weather (incessant rain, or, believe it or not, heatwaves), blisters, or simply a heavy pack day after day can all contribute to a sad experience. Seasoned hillwalkers should have little difficulty in taking the Coast to Coast Walk in their stride, but the less experienced should ensure they become 'more' experienced before venturing on a multi-day trek such as this: the Northern Hills are much in evidence!

USEFUL MAPS

The Coast to Coast Walk is covered on two specially prepared Harvey Maps at the scale of 1:40,000 (*Coast to Coast West, St Bees to Keld*, and *Coast to Coast East, Keld to Robin Hood's Bay*), and similarly by Footprint maps from Stirling Surveys, again split into *Coast to Coast West* and *Coast to Coast East*. Note that the set of two maps produced by the Ordnance Survey, Outdoor Leisure Maps *33 (St Bees to Keld)* and *34 (Keld to Robin Hood's Bay)* are no longer in print.

Extremely useful for finding exactly where you are in the great scheme of things are the OS Landranger sheets (1:50,000 scale), giving a complete picture of the neighbourhood of the walk and locations of potential alternative routes and other features. The following cover the route:

89 West Cumbria
90 Penrith, Keswick & Ambleside
91 Appleby in Westmorland
92 Barnard Castle
93 Middlesbrough & Darlington
94 Whitby
98 Wensleydale & Upper Wharfedale
99 Northallerton & Ripon

THE COUNTRY CODE

* Respect the life and work of the countryside
* Protect wildlife, plants and trees
* Keep to public paths across farmland
* Safeguard water supplies
* Go carefully on country roads
* Keep dogs under control
* Guard against all risks of fire
* Fasten all gates
* Leave no litter - take it with you
* Make no unnecessary noise
* Leave livestock, crops and machinery alone
* Use gates and stiles to cross fences, hedges and walls

Remember - paths can be created, diverted or even extinguished: please adhere to any legitimate notices you might encounter, which will be more recent and therefore take precedence over this guide.

A general guide only

	Youth Hostel	Accommodation	Camping	Bus service	Rail station	Pub	Post office	Other shop	WC	Phone	Cafe
St Bees		•	•	•	•	•	•	•	•	•	•
Sandwith		•	•			•				•	
Moor Row			•			•				•	
Cleator		•	•			•	•	•		•	•
Ennerdale Bridge		•	•	•		•	•			•	
Gillerthwaite	•	•	•							•	
Black Sail Hut	•										
Honister Pass	•			•							
Seatoller		•	•	•		•			•	•	•
Rosthwaite	•	•	•	•		•	•		•	•	
Stonethwaite		•	•			•				•	
Grasmere	•	•		•		•	•	•	•	•	•
Glenridding	•	•	•	•		•	•	•	•	•	•
Patterdale	•	•	•	•		•	•		•	•	
Burnbanks		•		•						•	
Bampton		•	•	•		•	•			•	•
Shap		•	•	•		•	•	•	•	•	•
Orton		•	•	•		•	•		•	•	•
Tebay	•	•	•	•		•	•		•	•	•
Raisbeck		•	•						•		
Newbiggin on Lune		•	•	•					•		
Ravenstonedale		•	•			•	•		•		
Kirkby Stephen	•	•	•	•	•	•	•	•	•	•	•
Hartley				•					•		
Keld	•	•	•	•					•	•	•
Muker		•	•			•	•	•	•	•	•
Gunnerside		•	•			•	•		•	•	•
Low Row		•	•	•		•	•		•	•	
Healaugh		•		•						•	
Reeth		•	•	•		•	•	•	•	•	•
Fremington		•	•	•							
Grinton	•	•	•	•		•				•	•

SOME USEFUL FACILITIES

A general guide only

	Youth Hostel	Accommodation	Camping	Bus service	Rail station	Pub	Post office	Other shop	WC	Phone	Cafe
Marrick		•	•							•	
Marske										•	•
Richmond		•	•	•		•	•	•		•	•
Colburn			•			•	•	•		•	
Brompton on Swale		•	•	•		•	•			•	
Catterick Bridge		•	•	•		•				•	•
Scorton			•			•	•	•		•	
Bolton on Swale		•	•							•	
Streetlam		•								•	
Danby Wiske		•	•	•		•				•	•
Oaktree Hill		•	•	•						•	
Ingleby Arncliffe		•						•			•
Ingleby Cross		•	•	•		•	•			•	
Osmotherley	•	•	•	•		•	•	•	•	•	
Swainby		•	•	•		•	•		•	•	
Huthwaite Green		•								•	
Carlton Bank									•	•	•
Carlton		•	•			•					
Cringle Moor		•	•								
Great Broughton		•	•			•	•	•		•	
Chop Gate		•	•	•		•			•	•	
Farndale Head		•	•							•	
Blakey		•	•	•							
Glaisdale		•	•		•	•	•		•	•	•
Egton Bridge		•		•	•	•			•	•	
Grosmont		•	•	•	•	•	•	•	•	•	•
Sleights		•		•	•	•	•		•	•	•
Littlebeck		•	•							•	
Hawsker		•	•	•		•	•			•	
Robin Hood's Bay	•	•	•	•		•	•	•	•	•	•

SOME USEFUL ADDRESSES

• COAST TO COAST SERVICES

The Coast to Coast Packhorse (transport)
Littlethwaite, North Stainmore, Kirkby Stephen CA17 4EX
Tel: 017683-42028   website: www.cumbria.com/packhorse

The White Knight (transport)
35 Cokeham Road, Lancing, West Sussex BN15 0AE
Tel: 01903-766475   E-mail: whiteknight@instep.demon.co.uk

Sherpa Van Project (transport)
131a Heston Road, Hounslow TW5 0RD   Tel. 0181-569 4101

Youth Hostels Association (accommodation bureau)
Trevelyan House, Dimple Rd, Matlock DE4 3YH   Tel. 01629-592600

Mrs. Whitehead (accommodation booklet)
Butt House, Keld, Richmond DL11 6LJ   Tel. 01748-886374

North York Moors Adventure Centre (accommodation booklet/souvenirs)
Park House, Ingleby Cross, Northallerton DL6 3PE   Tel: 01609-882571

Discovery Travel (guided/self-guided walks)
12 Towthorpe Rd, Haxby, York YO32 3ND   Tel: 01904-766564
Website: www.discoverytravel.co.uk

Spotlight website (Coast to Coast features):   www.coast2coast.co.uk

• ORGANISATIONS

Ramblers' Association
2nd Floor, Camelford House, 87-89 Albert Embankment, London SE1 7BR
Tel. 020-7339 8500

Friends of the Lake District
No.3, Yard 77, Highgate, Kendal LA9 4ED   Tel. 01539-720788

Yorkshire Dales Society
Otley Civic Centre, Cross Green, Otley LS21 1HD   Tel. 01943-461938

North Yorkshire Moors Association Honorary Secretary:
Angulon House, Bank Lane, Faceby TS9 7BP

• INFORMATION - TOURIST BOARDS, NATIONAL PARKS

Cumbria Tourist Board
Ashleigh, Holly Road, Windermere, Cumbria LA23 2AQ
Tel. 015394-44444

Yorkshire Tourist Board
312 Tadcaster Road, York YO2 2HF
Tel. 01904-707961

Lake District National Park Visitor Services
Brockhole, Windermere, Cumbria LA23 1LJ
Tel. 015394-46601

Yorkshire Dales National Park Information Services
Colvend, Hebden Road, Grassington, Skipton BD23 5LB
Tel. 01756-752748

North York Moors National Park Information Service
The Old Vicarage, Bondgate, Helmsley, York YO6 5BP
Tel. 01439-770657

• INFORMATION - ON OR NEAR THE WALK

Whitehaven Tourist Information
Market Hall, Market Place, Whitehaven, Cumbria CA28 7JG
Tel. 01946-852939

Egremont Tourist Information
12 Main Street, Egremont, Cumbria, CA22 2DW
Tel. 01946-820693

Seatoller National Park Information
Seatoller Barn, Seatoller, Keswick, Cumbria CA12 5XN
Tel. 017687-77294

Keswick National Park Information
The Moot Hall, Market Square, Keswick, Cumbria CA12 5JR
Tel. 017687-72645

Grasmere National Park Information
Redbank Road, Grasmere, Ambleside, Cumbria LA22 9SW
Tel. 015394-35245

Glenridding National Park Information
Main Car Park, Glenridding, Penrith, Cumbria CA11 0PA
Tel. 017684-82414

Kirkby Stephen Tourist Information
Market Street, Kirkby Stephen, Cumbria CA17 4QN
Tel. 017683-71199

Reeth National Park Information
Hudson House, Reeth, Richmond DL11 6TB
Tel. 01748-884059

Richmond Tourist Information
Friary Gardens, Victoria Road, Richmond, N Yorks. DL10 4AJ
Tel. 01748-850252

Northallerton Tourist Information
The Applegarth, Northallerton, North Yorkshire DL7 8LZ
Tel. 01609-776864

The Moors Centre, Danby Lodge
Lodge Lane, Danby, Whitby, North Yorkshire YO21 2NB
Tel. 01287-660654

Whitby Tourist Information
Langborne Road, Whitby, North Yorkshire YO21 1YN
Tel. 01947-602674

Scarborough Tourist Information
Pavilion House, Valley Bridge Rd, Scarborough, N Yorks YO11 1UZ
Tel. 01723-373333

• *PUBLIC TRANSPORT*

Traveline: Tel. 0870-608 2608

National Rail Enquiry Line: Tel. 08457-484950

THE ROUTE GUIDE

The main body of this book is a detailed guide to the walk itself, extending from page 20 to page 139. It is divided into twelve sections, each having its own introduction: these are quickly located by reference to the contents on page 5. Each introduction includes a gradient profile of the route (vertical scale greatly exaggerated) and a summary of the walking, along with suggestions for alternatives to the main route. Many are the result of personal exploration, and can all be plotted from the Landranger maps.

A continuous strip-map runs throughout the guide, accompanied by a narrative of the route. Remaining space is then devoted to notes and illustrations of features of interest along the way.

Key to the map symbols

ST BEES to ENNERDALE BRIDGE

14 miles   *1900 feet of ascent*

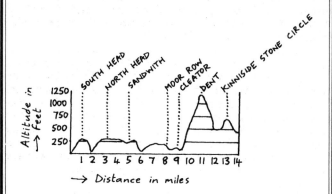

The opening day offers three well defined sections, though in this sandwich the filling is the least appetising part. That rare creature the Cumbrian clifftop provides an outstanding introduction to the walk, several airy miles of tall sea cliffs putting one in the perfect frame of mind for a near-200 mile walk. On leaving the coast there follow several miles that are interesting but unexciting, as a corner of the ill-fated West Cumberland industrial belt is traversed. Ahead, however, are the hills, and beyond Cleator the unassuming little fell of Dent is, despite afforestation, a foretaste of Lakeland.

Alternatives, other than short-cuts, are few: this day is more circuitous than most, and an obvious bee-line for Ennerdale Bridge can be plotted. Other than a path climbing from St Bees to Loughrigg Farm however, road walking dominates the short-cut. The two great natural features of the walk are both time consuming, though only in desperation should St Bees Head be omitted: there's nothing like it for a long time! If flagging, the back road from Cleator to Ennerdale Bridge avoids Dent.

When the great moment arrives, and you're stood on the sea wall facing the Irish Sea, ensure the first task is completed by dipping at least a toe into its waters before heading for the cliffs. The sea wall ends abruptly where a footbridge crosses Rottington Beck and a sign points to St Bees Head and Fleswick Bay. Additional signs advise of the presence of an RSPB nature reserve and dangerous cliffs, both of significance. Ascent to the clifftops is by way of a steep flight of wooden steps, after which it's easy going up aloft for an inspiring introduction to the Coast to Coast Walk. A clear day carries the immediate bonus of extensive views inland to the mountains of Wasdale.

ST BEES is an intriguing village, rich in historical interest but also attractive in its own right, even without its backdrop of the headland (see overleaf). The name of St. Bega is the recurring link from the earliest times to the present day. The Priory Church gives her shared billing in its dedication, for back in 650 AD this Irish princess established a nunnery here. Destroyed by the Danes, the site breathed new life as a priory in about 1120, by Benedictine monks from York. The strikingly beautiful west doorway (illustrated on page 1) remains intact from the priory's early years.

Also famous is the grammar school, which itself dates back over four centuries. Aside from the obligatory modern attachments, the heart of the village is a long, straggling main street lined with a varied collection of buildings. The railway from Whitehaven opened in 1849, and as a fortunate survivor it plays an important role 'way out west'.

scant remains of a
coastguard lookout

Pattering
Holes
ruin

modern
housing

WHITEHAVEN
B5345

Cumbrian Coast Line

P

S

sea
wall

hotel
cafe

St Bees

beach

Cumbrian R.

Main St.

EGREMONT
B5345

IRISH
SEA

THE
START

C - car park/wc
L - Lifeboat
P - Priory Church
S - School
R - Railway station

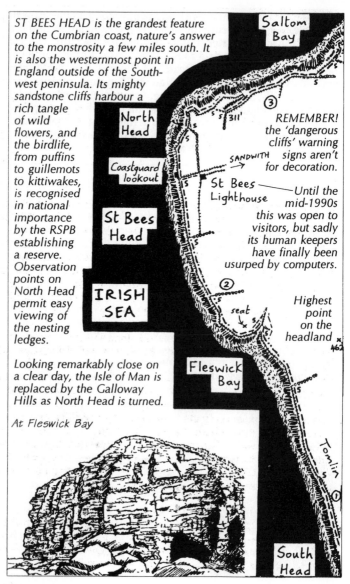

ST BEES HEAD is the grandest feature on the Cumbrian coast, nature's answer to the monstrosity a few miles south. It is also the westernmost point in England outside of the Southwest peninsula. Its mighty sandstone cliffs harbour a rich tangle of wild flowers, and the birdlife, from puffins to guillemots to kittiwakes, is recognised in national importance by the RSPB establishing a reserve. Observation points on North Head permit easy viewing of the nesting ledges.

Looking remarkably close on a clear day, the Isle of Man is replaced by the Galloway Hills as North Head is turned.

At Fleswick Bay

Saltom Bay

North Head

Coastguard lookout

St Bees Head

IRISH SEA

③

REMEMBER! the 'dangerous cliffs' warning signs aren't for decoration.

SANDWITH

St Bees Lighthouse —Until the mid-1990s this was open to visitors, but sadly its human keepers have finally been usurped by computers.

311'

②

seat

Highest point on the headland

462

Fleswick Bay

Tomlin

①

South Head

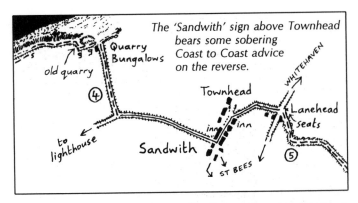

The 'Sandwith' sign above Townhead bears some sobering Coast to Coast advice on the reverse.

After a long time on the seaward side of the fence on South Head, the path transfers over for a steady drop to the prominent inlet of Fleswick Bay. The path descends to within a few feet of sea level before regaining height for the longer march atop North Head, though many will be tempted to venture onto the shore. Here are cliffs, flowers, birds, caves, waterworn rocks, and a dazzling array of smooth pebbles underfoot. The path can be regained by locating a series of holds in the rock to a hurdle above, avoiding having to go inland to the main stile.

Forging on below the lighthouse and alongside the lookout, the path is soon returned in dramatic fashion to the clifftop around the point of North Head. Ahead, Saltom Bay laps the Whitehaven shoreline, with the harbour entrance visible. Within a couple of minutes the path re-crosses to the safer side of the fence, crossing the field to a stile to resume above higher level 'inland' cliffs. This curious feature is replicated on several occasions just here, including a section where the path itself runs a narrow course between rock walls. Though remaining largely on the seaward side, landslips have forced a section of path into the field-side. The end of the cliff walk comes as a shock on emerging above the former Birkhams Quarry, a right mess!

At the cottages turn inland on a rough lane sunken between hedgerows, then left at a junction with the lighthouse road to enter Sandwith. Turn left in the village, curving up to the right past the *Dog & Partridge* to a junction at Lanehead. Cross straight over to run the full length of a gem of a green byway.

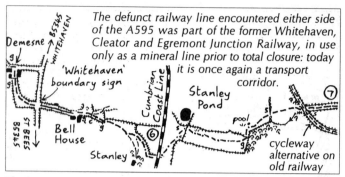

The defunct railway line encountered either side of the A595 was part of the former Whitehaven, Cleator and Egremont Junction Railway, in use only as a mineral line prior to total closure: today it is once again a transport corridor.

The byway runs on to Demesne, turning right through the farmyard and out on a rough track onto the B5345 Whitehaven-St Bees road. Cross over and along the farm road to Bell House. Keep on past it to a cattle-grid on a brow, with a splendid prospect ahead beyond Stanley Pond. As the track forks on descent, bear right to a gate, then trend left down a thinner branch towards another gate, but keeping on down the field-side to a railway underpass.

On the other side bear left to a stile in the far corner. A faint path crosses a long enclosure towards a wood, escaping by a gate on the left before swinging right to climb two fields to a rail underpass (now converted to the West Cumbria Cycle Path, this offers an alternative route to Moor Row). An enclosed track climbs to meet the A595 Whitehaven-Egremont road. Cross and go straight along Scalegill Road. Either advance on to the end, or use a new variation left along a driveway just before the old rail bridge. At the houses a footpath takes over to quickly join the former line. Follow this surfaced cycleway just two minutes under a bridge, then turn right up onto the road on the edge of Moor Row. Head along by the long terraces of Dalzell Street to a junction by the Post office, and keep straight on to quickly leave the village.

Over a brow the leafy lane is vacated by a kissing-gate on the left, and after a brief rise, a path slants right, down to cross another converted line. It continues on a link route towards Cleator, just ahead. With a well-tended cricket ground in front, the path joins the head of a lane to enter Cleator's main street. Go left a short way to a shop in a terrace, and turn down Kiln Brow opposite. At the bottom go right at a housing development to Blackhow Bridge over the Ehen, from where a rough byway climbs away.

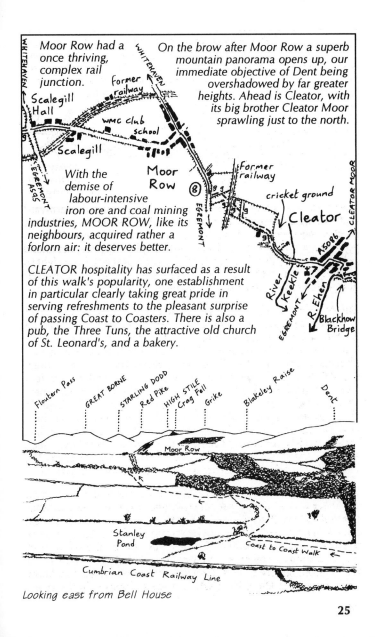

Moor Row had a once thriving, complex rail junction.

On the brow after Moor Row a superb mountain panorama opens up, our immediate objective of Dent being overshadowed by far greater heights. Ahead is Cleator, with its big brother Cleator Moor sprawling just to the north.

WHITEHAVEN

Scalegill Hall

Former railway

wmc club

school

Scalegill

Moor Row

⑧

Former railway

cricket ground

Cleator

CLEATOR MOOR

EGREMONT A595

With the demise of labour-intensive iron ore and coal mining industries, MOOR ROW, like its neighbours, acquired rather a forlorn air: it deserves better.

EGREMONT

A5086

CLEATOR hospitality has surfaced as a result of this walk's popularity, one establishment in particular clearly taking great pride in serving refreshments to the pleasant surprise of passing Coast to Coasters. There is also a pub, the Three Tuns, the attractive old church of St. Leonard's, and a bakery.

River Keekle

EGREMONT

R. Ehen

Blackhow Bridge

Floutern Pass   GREAT BORNE   STARLING DODD   Red Pike   HIGH STILE   Crag Fell   Grike   Blakeley Raise   Dent

Moor Row

Stanley Pond

Coast to Coast Walk

Cumbrian Coast Railway Line

Looking east from Bell House

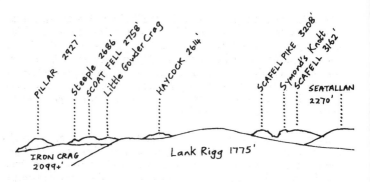

PILLAR 2927'
Steeple 2686'
SCOAT FELL 2758'
Little Gowder Crag
HAYCOCK 2614'
SCAFELL PIKE 3208
Symond's Knott
SCAFELL 3162'
SEATALLAN 2270'
IRON CRAG 2099+'
Lank Rigg 1775'

The Lakeland Fells from Dent
(the Scafell peaks are 11 miles distant)

First stage of the ascent of Dent, the lane works up the slope to Black How Farm, passing round the nearside of the buildings to emerge on a road. This provides the quickest means, at this stage, of reaching Ennerdale Bridge if the situation becomes desperate.

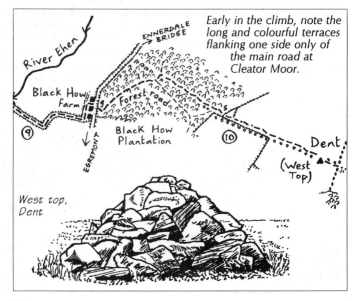

River Ehen

ENNERDALE BRIDGE

Early in the climb, note the long and colourful terraces flanking one side only of the main road at Cleator Moor.

Black How Farm

Forest road

Black How Plantation

EGREMONT

⑨

⑩

Dent (West Top)

West top, Dent

The gate opposite gives access to Black How Plantation, which has buried the open fellside without trace. A forest road doubles back up to the left with far-reaching views over the West Cumberland plain. When some height has been gained, a guide-post sends a path 50 yards off to the left to resume a parallel climb on a far more accommodating surface. The pleasant path soon breaks free of the plantations, maintaining its straight line to arrive at the big cairn atop Dent.

This is only the traditional summit and not the true one, which is found across the marshy depression to the east. Though possessing the most diminutive of cairns, the highest point claims the distinct advantage of turning its back on the plain in favour of its grandstand setting for Lakeland's western skyline, at the heart of which is the deep enclave of Ennerdale to be penetrated on the next stage of the journey. This is a superb wilderness panorama stretching from Hopegill Head through Grasmoor, High Stile, Pillar and the Scafells to the Black Combe ridge.

Descend to a stile in a fence, quickly entering trees to run down as a broad path, over a minor crossroads to reach a junction with a forest road. Go left and within 100 yards take a stile in the fence ahead, to gain a breath of fresh air on the contrastingly open eastern shoulder of the fell. A clear path runs to the far end to drop uncomfortably steeply to Nannycatch Beck. Turn left on the path through this narrow and immensely pleasant little valley, over a brace of footbridges and a stile at Nannycatch Gate.

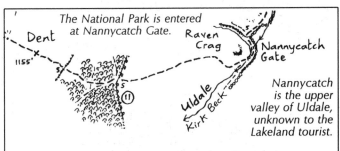

The National Park is entered at Nannycatch Gate.

Dent
1155'

Raven Crag

Nannycatch Gate

Uldale Beck
Kirk

Nannycatch is the upper valley of Uldale, unknown to the Lakeland tourist.

Although the 1994 OS route map depicts a different line of descent from the plantation east of the summit, waymarking in 1997 very firmly points the walk along the original and more direct route, as shown here.

Passing below Flatfell Screes up to the left, the beck fades but the clear path bears right to work steadily up towards the open fell road. A branch path doubles back right to visit Kinniside Stone Circle, which well merits an inspection: if keeping on to the end, then turn briefly right on the narrow farm road to join the fell road. Go left along the road for a steady descent to Ennerdale Bridge, enjoying the parade of mountains as a finale to this stage. At the bottom turn right for the village.

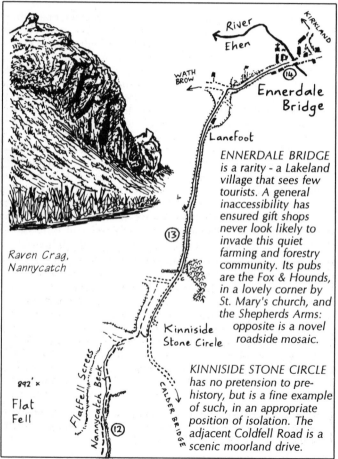

River Ehen

KIRKLAND

WATH BROW

Ennerdale Bridge

114

Lanefoot

13

ENNERDALE BRIDGE is a rarity - a Lakeland village that sees few tourists. A general inaccessibility has ensured gift shops never look likely to invade this quiet farming and forestry community. Its pubs are the Fox & Hounds, in a lovely corner by St. Mary's church, and the Shepherds Arms: opposite is a novel roadside mosaic.

Raven Crag, Nannycatch

Kinniside Stone Circle

KINNISIDE STONE CIRCLE has no pretension to pre-history, but is a fine example of such, in an appropriate position of isolation. The adjacent Coldfell Road is a scenic moorland drive.

892′ ×

Flat Fell

Flatfell Screes

Nannycatch Beck

CALDER BRIDGE

12

28

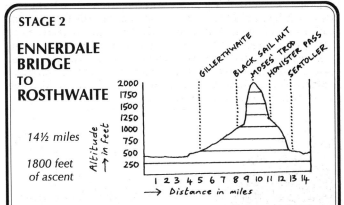

STAGE 2

ENNERDALE BRIDGE TO ROSTHWAITE

14½ miles

1800 feet of ascent

Altitude → in feet

2000
1750
1500
1250
1000
750
500
250

GILLERTHWAITE
BLACK SAIL HUT
MOSES' TROD
HONISTER PASS
SEATOLLER

1 2 3 4 5 6 7 8 9 10 11 12 13 14
→ Distance in miles

Another triple-section day comprising lakeshore, forest and mountainside, as a tramp the length of Ennerdale precedes a crossing into the head of Borrowdale. The opening miles are a splendid ramble along the entire southern shore of Ennerdale Water. While the higher reaches of the dale are draped in the dark green of forestry, progress is rapid on a broad track giving glimpses up to the surrounding fells. Beyond Black Sail Hut the open air might have come off a prescription as, faced by high-walled mountains, the inevitable climb brings fresh views and a varied descent on broad paths into Borrowdale.

There are no shorter alternatives, but a host of more adventurous routes. All involve serious fellwalking, and other than the first mentioned, are best left to the strong and experienced, certainly at such an early stage of a long walk. The least arduous fellwalking alternative leaves the valley road where indicated for Scarth Gap, and from the pass a well-worn path climbs to the summit of Haystacks, continuing on less obvious paths to Moses' Trod. This route takes on a certain poignancy in view of the great man's final resting place. Higher level options include the High Stile ridge lining the valley to the north and signposted from Gillerthwaite; and an ascent of Great Gable from the dalehead, then continuing north to Moses' Trod or descending to Seathwaite for Seatoller.

Variations near the outset would be to use the north shore path and forest road to the head of the lake; and the forest road south of the river as far as the Pillar footbridge.

Leave the village by the Croasdale Road, turning right for the lake where indicated on a zigzag road that expires upon crossing the river Ehen. Go left past a second car park on the site of a pumping station, on a broad track to the foot of Ennerdale Water. Here turn right along the south shore footpath. This runs undeviatingly along the length of the lake, always within yards of the water's edge. High up to the right in the early stages the fangs of Crag Fell Pinnacles tower menacingly above, while the individual highlight is the scrambly crossing of the base of Anglers' Crag, which plummets directly into the water.

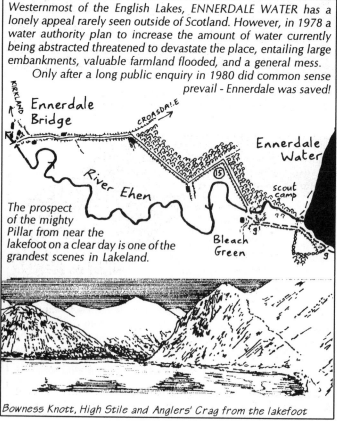

Westernmost of the English Lakes, ENNERDALE WATER has a lonely appeal rarely seen outside of Scotland. However, in 1978 a water authority plan to increase the amount of water currently being abstracted threatened to devastate the place, entailing large embankments, valuable farmland flooded, and a general mess.
Only after a long public enquiry in 1980 did common sense prevail - Ennerdale was saved!

KIRKLAND

Ennerdale
Bridge

CROASDALE

Ennerdale
Water

River Ehen

scout
camp

The prospect
of the mighty
Pillar from near the
lakefoot on a clear day is one of the
grandest scenes in Lakeland.

Bleach
Green

Bowness Knott, High Stile and Anglers' Crag from the lakefoot

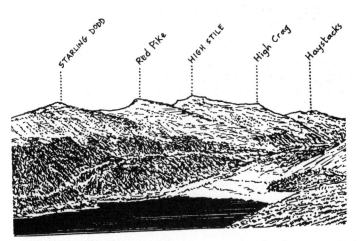

The high mountain wall enclosing the north side of Ennerdale, seen from the slopes of Crag Fell

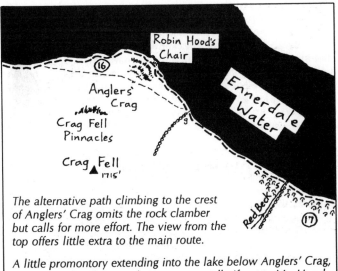

The alternative path climbing to the crest of Anglers' Crag omits the rock clamber but calls for more effort. The view from the top offers little extra to the main route.

A little promontory extending into the lake below Anglers' Crag, Robin Hood's Chair is relevant to our walk, if not to Mr. Hood.

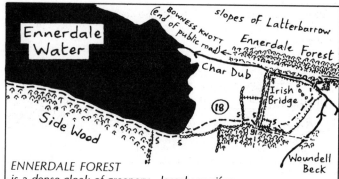

ENNERDALE FOREST
*is a dense cloak of greenery - largely coniferous -
that sits uneasily over the entire valley between lake and dalehead.
Established for increased timber demands after the First World War,
it suffocates the heart of Lakeland's remotest valley. In recent times
the Forestry Commission has laid out several trails, and is showing
a willingness to implement some diversity of species.*

The second half of the lakeside walk runs through the wonderfully natural Side Wood, a section to be savoured in view of the
forest stage imminent. From a stile at the end take the right-hand
green swath through the bracken in this dead flat strath at the
lake-head. At the second wall a forest road is joined, presenting
a choice of either going left with it to join the valley road (the
simplest option), or following it into the forest, briefly, turning
immediately left and within 100 yards left again to leave by a stile
on the left. Aim half-right across the field for a footbridge over
the Liza, and from the stile in the corner opposite, rise to meet
the valley road.

Turn right along the road, which passes Low Gillerthwaite (a field
centre) and High Gillerthwaite (a youth hostel) where it loses its
surface. The forest road forges on over a cattle-grid deep into the
trees, at the same time as a high-level ridgewalk option takes
advantage of the break on the left. So, through the forest we go,
undeflected by lesser branches or forks. Various felled sections
permit more open views to the high fells. When the great
mountains reveal themselves, outstanding is the increasingly
powerful outline of Pillar Rock, high up to the right.

Five minutes beyond High Gillerthwaite the High Stile alternative, via Red Pike, High Stile and Haystacks, departs from the valley as a sheep-droving break.

Ennerdale Forest

Low Gillerthwaite ⑲ High Gillerthwaite ⑳

River Liza

Pillar Rock from the forest road. Low cloud on Pillar reveals the majestic tower that gave the mountain its name

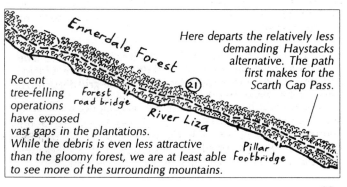

Ennerdale Forest

⑳

Forest road bridge ㉑

River Liza

Here departs the relatively less demanding Haystacks alternative. The path first makes for the Scarth Gap Pass.

Recent tree-felling operations have exposed vast gaps in the plantations.

Pillar Footbridge

While the debris is even less attractive than the gloomy forest, we are at least able to see more of the surrounding mountains.

33

The hard road eventually reaches the end of the forest, and as it swings down to the right, take the gate in front with a glimpse of Black Sail Hut, and even better, Great Gable, behind it. The path runs broadly on to the youth hostel. After a sojourn in the open spaces of the dalehead, overlooked by Pillar, Kirk Fell and Gable, the main path runs down to a footbridge over the Liza: without crossing, turn upstream to the inflowing Loft Beck, which is followed away. Better, however, to turn a few feet up behind the hut to find the start of a contouring trod. This gradually becomes clearer to enjoy a splendid traverse to reach unmistakeable Loft Beck, only yards above its merger with Tongue Beck. On crossing it a well-worn (eroded, in part) path begins an immediate ascent of its bank, climbing steeply between heather-covered flanks.

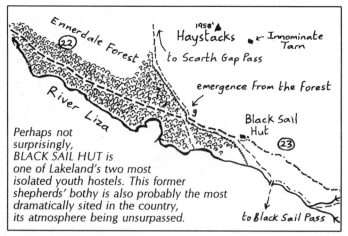

Perhaps not surprisingly, BLACK SAIL HUT is one of Lakeland's two most isolated youth hostels. This former shepherds' bothy is also probably the most dramatically sited in the country, its atmosphere being unsurpassed.

At the top a line of small cairns escorts the path up easier ground, with Crummock Water and the slaty Grasmoor Fells appearing across to the left: note also the great near-vertical north wall of Haystacks, closer to hand. The old Ennerdale boundary fence is crossed during its climb to the summit of Brandreth up to the right, while our path motors on its gentler way. Soon the Moses' Trod path will be espied contouring around the flank of Grey Knotts ahead, our path being set on a collision course with it. At the junction go left along the broad way of the Trod, with the great wet hollow of Warnscale Bottom down to the left, and the outspread Buttermere Valley making a memorable scene.

Black Sail Hut, looking to Green Gable and Great Gable

On the pull by LOFT BECK, the long awaited first view out of Ennerdale is a sighting of Red Pike (Wasdale) over Black Sail Pass. This is followed by Scafell over Beck Head. On easing round, Haystacks appears to the left, backed by High Crag.

Dubs Bottom

Grey Knotts
△
2286'

BRANDRETH
▲
2345'

24

1970'

Moses' Trod

Loft Beck

Tongue Beck

River Liza

As can be gleaned from their proximity to the route, the summits of both BRANDRETH and its lesser underling Grey Knotts might be claimed as a 'late in the day' bonus if conditions prove suitable. This ridge falling to Honister Pass is the northerly extension of Great Gable.

MOSES' TROD is a spanking walkers' route through the hills, but did not originate as such. This old way from the quarries above Honister to Wasdale Head (and onward to the coast at Ravenglass) was established for the passage of packhorses laden with slate. Its name recalls one of the great characters of the Honister quarries, whose supposed spare-time occupation of distilling and smuggling whisky gave him further cause to travel this way.

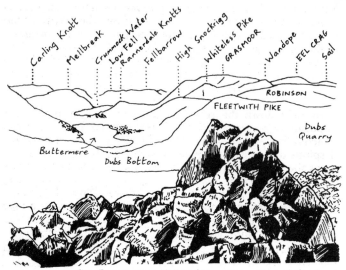

Carling Knott · Mellbreak · Crummock Water · Low Fell · Rannerdale Knotts · Fellbarrow · High Snockrigg · Whiteless Pike · GRASMOOR · Wandope · EEL CRAG · Sail

ROBINSON
FLEETWITH PIKE

Dubs Quarry

Buttermere · Dubs Bottom

The Buttermere Valley from above Moses' Trod

HONISTER PASS is one of Lakeland's better known road passes. Part of its popularity is the ease with which it forms part of a circular tour from Keswick, a facility taken full advantage of well before the advent of the motor car, when trips by waggonette were hampered by passengers being forced to get out and walk the steeper sections! The former toll road gives an ideal escape from the traffic, being better graded and affording spectacular views over the mountains encircling the dalehead. While the hinterland of Honister Crag openly displays all the scars of quarrying, its sombre face is riddled with tunnels and shafts from the hard days spent prising out slate - days that only quite recently passed into history.

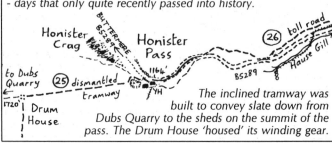

Honister Crag · BUTTERMERE B5289 · Honister Pass · toll road · (26) · House Gill

to Dubs Quarry · (25) dismantled tramway · 1164' · YH · B5289

1720' · Drum House

The inclined tramway was built to convey slate down from Dubs Quarry to the sheds on the summit of the pass. The Drum House 'housed' its winding gear.

36

The trod runs down to another major junction at the conspicuous remains of the Drum House. Go right down the course of the dismantled tramway that runs unerringly from the Drum House to the former quarry sheds on the summit of Honister Pass. This is a popular motorists' halt, though the sudden population boom is tempered by the remarkable revelation of Honister Crag falling to the pass on its descent towards Gatesgarth.

Turn right down the road a short way, though at the first opportunity its verges are left in favour of the old Honister road, which rather cleverly keeps generally clear of the motor road as it spirals down to Borrowdale, concluding through the enclosures above Seatoller. Go left through the tiny village, leaving by a stile at the end of the car park. Keeping right at an initial fork, a charming path runs on above the Derwent through Johnny's Wood, terminating at Longthwaite youth hostel. Cross the bridge over the river, and a few yards up the road a path breaks off to the left to run more directly through the fields to Rosthwaite.

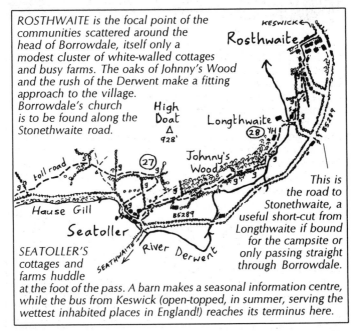

ROSTHWAITE is the focal point of the communities scattered around the head of Borrowdale, itself only a modest cluster of white-walled cottages and busy farms. The oaks of Johnny's Wood and the rush of the Derwent make a fitting approach to the village. Borrowdale's church is to be found along the Stonethwaite road.

KESWICK

Rosthwaite

High Doat
△ 928'

Longthwaite

(28) YH!

B5289

Johnny's Wood

toll road

(27)

Hause Gill

B5289

Seatoller

SEATOLLER'S cottages and farms huddle

River Derwent

SEATHWAITE

This is the road to Stonethwaite, a useful short-cut from Longthwaite if bound for the campsite or only passing straight through Borrowdale.

at the foot of the pass. A barn makes a seasonal information centre, while the bus from Keswick (open-topped, in summer, serving the wettest inhabited places in England!) reaches its terminus here.

ROSTHWAITE TO PATTERDALE

17½ miles

4000 feet of ascent

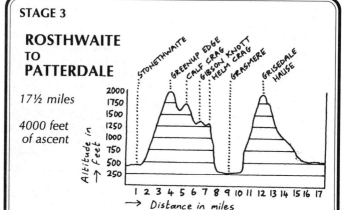

This section walks very much against the grain, being faced by a pair of north-south ridges ranged against attempts at easterly progress. Clear paths make use of passes in each instance, though as both the Central Ridge and the Helvellyn-Fairfield ridge must be crossed at virtually the 2000ft contour, the prospect of this dual 'ascent' usually encourages an overnight halt at Grasmere. The valley scenery at each end (Stonethwaite and Grisedale) is matched by the intervening loveliness of the Vale of Grasmere.

Settling for Grasmere gives chance to incorporate high summits into one or both days. With experience and weather on your side, options to Grasmere include Stonethwaite to Greenup Edge by way of Dock Tarn and Ullscarf, or leaving Greenup Edge for High Raise and Easedale Tarn. A longer Stonethwaite option goes by way of Langstrath, Stake Pass, Langdale Pikes and Blea Rigg for Easedale and Grasmere. In contrast, the direct route from Far Easedale Head down to Grasmere short-cuts the main route. Beyond Grasmere higher mountains are the only alternatives, being departures from Grisedale Tarn either onto Saint Sunday Crag (not too demanding) or Helvellyn, a stiffer proposition.

If still bent on completing the section in one day, then there is little point in descending all the way to Grasmere's valley level. Instead, drop into Wythburn to meet the A591 above Thirlmere, then up by Dunmail Raise to follow Raise Beck to Grisedale Tarn.

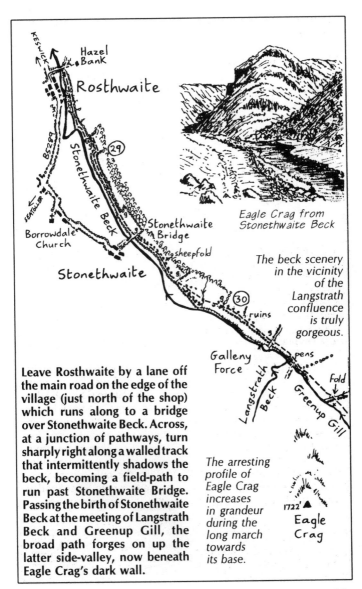

Hazel Bank

Rosthwaite

KESWICK

B5289

SEATOLLER

Stonethwaite Beck

29

Borrowdale Church

Stonethwaite Bridge

Stonethwaite

sheepfold

30

ruins

Eagle Crag from Stonethwaite Beck

The beck scenery in the vicinity of the Langstrath confluence is truly gorgeous.

Galleny Force

pens

Langstrath Beck

Greenup Gill

Fold

Leave Rosthwaite by a lane off the main road on the edge of the village (just north of the shop) which runs along to a bridge over Stonethwaite Beck. Across, at a junction of pathways, turn sharply right along a walled track that intermittently shadows the beck, becoming a field-path to run past Stonethwaite Bridge. Passing the birth of Stonethwaite Beck at the meeting of Langstrath Beck and Greenup Gill, the broad path forges on up the latter side-valley, now beneath Eagle Crag's dark wall.

The arresting profile of Eagle Crag increases in grandeur during the long march towards its base.

1722' ▲

Eagle Crag

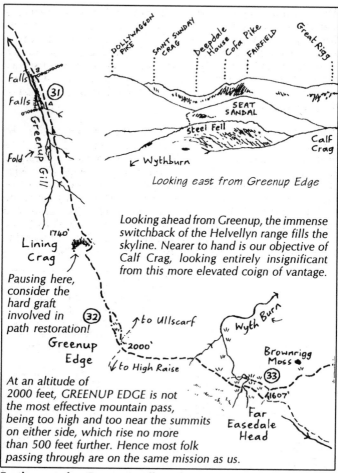

DOLLYWAGGON PIKE · SAINT SUNDAY CRAG · Deepdale Hause · Cofa Pike · FAIRFIELD · Great Rigg

SEAT SANDAL

Steel Fell

← Wythburn

Calf Crag

Looking east from Greenup Edge

Looking ahead from Greenup, the immense switchback of the Helvellyn range fills the skyline. Nearer to hand is our objective of Calf Crag, looking entirely insignificant from this more elevated coign of vantage.

Falls

Falls

Fold

Greenup Gill

1740'
Lining Crag

Pausing here, consider the hard graft involved in path restoration!

Greenup Edge

↑ to Ullscarf

2000'

↓ to High Raise

Wyth Burn

Brownrigg Moss

1607'

Far Easedale Head

At an altitude of 2000 feet, GREENUP EDGE is not the most effective mountain pass, being too high and too near the summits on either side, which rise no more than 500 feet further. Hence most folk passing through are on the same mission as us.

Further up the Greenup valley, the path leaves the final wall behind and rises towards the imposing Lining Crag. Through clusters of drumlins the path arrives at the foot of the crag, then climbs adventurously to its left on a restored path. The top of the crag is an amiable green knoll few will pass without a detour, particularly as the next half-hour is much less auspicious: in any case, this is the place to bid farewell to Borrowdale.

Above Lining Crag the gradients relent, and in moist surroundings the cairned path runs on to the summit of the pass on Greenup Edge. The next pass, at Far Easedale Head, is clearly in view several hundred feet below, beyond the head of the intervening valley of Wythburn. The path thereto descends sharply before running across a marshy shelf, a deviation left being an alternative to the main path, which meets the crest of the pass at a redundant stile.

While the main path heads directly into Far Easedale in the company of the beck, the recommended route takes advantage of height gained to incorporate an extremely easy and hugely rewarding ridgewalk. Along to the left the undulating ridge climbs to Calf Crag, a short-half mile distant, then down and over the crest of Gibson Knott to the prominent Helm Crag out at the end. The short climb to Calf Crag soon reaches its cairned top above a steep fall to Easedale, before the path winds along to the cairned top of Gibson Knott. Note that the path does not slavishly adhere to the crest, preferring to savour the Easedale flank.

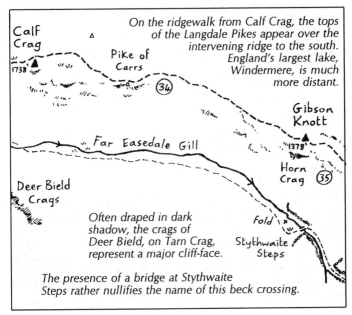

On the ridgewalk from Calf Crag, the tops of the Langdale Pikes appear over the intervening ridge to the south. England's largest lake, Windermere, is much more distant.

Calf Crag

Pike of Carrs

1738

Gibson Knott

Far Easedale Gill

1378

Horn Crag (35)

Deer Bield Crags

Often draped in dark shadow, the crags of Deer Bield, on Tarn Crag, represent a major cliff-face.

fold

Stythwaite Steps

The presence of a bridge at Stythwaite Steps rather nullifies the name of this beck crossing.

The short descent to the next saddle, Bracken Hause, precedes a final pull to Helm Crag, to be greeted by a knob of rock marking the summit. The path runs along Helm Crag's fascinating crest to similarly appointed outcrops at the other end before then commencing a pulsating descent towards the outspread Vale of Grasmere. After a short drop the path runs onto a green knoll, and here turn sharp right on a path that has replaced the erosion-stricken one continuing down the ridge-end. This well-made substitute winds down rather more sedately to meet the valley path in Far Easedale, turning left to quickly become surfaced. This access road heads out through a field and threads a long, pleasant, winding course to Grasmere village.

Summit rocks, Helm Crag

The summit of HELM CRAG is a bewildering wonderland that repays a careful exploration. The tilted tower of rock pointing skyward is best known as the Howitzer, and demands an adventurous scramble to claim a true ascent of Helm Crag.

Dove Cottage

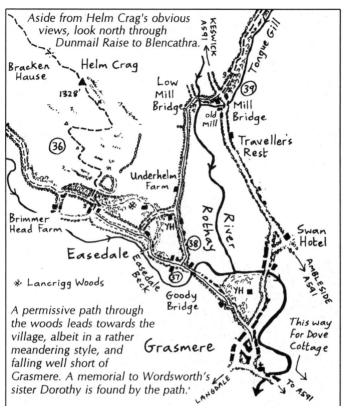

Aside from Helm Crag's obvious views, look north through Dunmail Raise to Blencathra.

Bracken Hause

Helm Crag

1328'

36

KESWICK A591

Tongue Gill

Low Mill Bridge

old mill

Mill Bridge

39

Traveller's Rest

Underhelm Farm

River Rothay

Brimmer Head Farm

YH

38

Swan Hotel

AMBLESIDE A591

Easedale

Easedale Beck

37

* Lancrigg Woods

Goody Bridge

YH

This way for Dove Cottage

A permissive path through the woods leads towards the village, albeit in a rather meandering style, and falling well short of Grasmere. A memorial to Wordsworth's sister Dorothy is found by the path.

Grasmere

LANGDALE

TO A591

GRASMERE is famous on two counts, its natural beauty and its literary connections. Gracing its own verdant vale, the physical attributes leave nothing to the imagination. The river Rothay flows into Grasmere's own sheet of water, a quiet mere disturbed only by rowing boats. Thronged with tourists from around the globe, the village centre is supported by several hamlets along the main road. It is one of these, Town End, that hides Dove Cottage, best known of William Wordsworth's Lakeland homes. The poet rests in the village churchyard, marked by the plainest of headstones. Other attractions at Grasmere include two famous annual events, the sports and the rushbearing, also a gingerbread shop, bookshop, and the Heaton Cooper gallery.

43

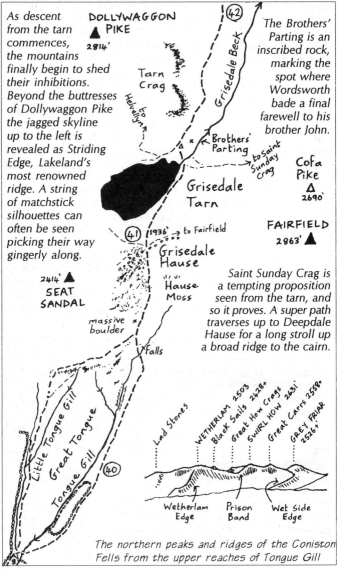

As descent from the tarn commences, the mountains finally begin to shed their inhibitions. Beyond the buttresses of Dollywaggon Pike the jagged skyline up to the left is revealed as Striding Edge, Lakeland's most renowned ridge. A string of matchstick silhouettes can often be seen picking their way gingerly along.

DOLLYWAGGON PIKE
2814'

Tarn Crag

to Helvellyn

Grisedale Beck

The Brothers' Parting is an inscribed rock, marking the spot where Wordsworth bade a final farewell to his brother John.

Brothers' Parting

to Saint Sunday Crag

Cofa Pike
△ 2690'

Grisedale Tarn

FAIRFIELD
2863' ▲

1936' → to Fairfield

2414' ▲
SEAT SANDAL

Grisedale Hause

Hause Moss

Saint Sunday Crag is a tempting proposition seen from the tarn, and so it proves. A super path traverses up to Deepdale Hause for a long stroll up a broad ridge to the cairn.

massive boulder

Falls

Little Tongue Gill

Great Tongue

Tongue Gill

Lad Stones
WETHERLAM 2503'
Black Sails 2628'+
Great How Crags 2628'+
SWIRL HOW 2631'
Great Carrs 2558'+
GREY FRIAR 2526'+

Wetherlam Edge   Prison Band   Wet Side Edge

The northern peaks and ridges of the Coniston Fells from the upper reaches of Tongue Gill

44

Departure from Grasmere (see previous map) is along the side-road leaving Easedale Road at Goody Bridge for Thorney How youth hostel, continuing on to a junction and then right, up to the A591 at Mill Bridge. Cross straight over the busy road and up a time-honoured track faithfully signposted to Patterdale.

When it gains the open fell a choice awaits, for paths run either side of Great Tongue, directly in front, to rejoin much higher up. The left-hand one is the broad green way of an old pony track, a super path now largely forgotten. The other, beginning from the footbridge to the right, is a more popular walkers' alternative. They meet under the abrupt eastern bluff of Seat Sandal, in readiness for gaining the top of Grisedale Hause. This is a fine moment, with the tarn immediately below and the unremitting wall of Dollywaggon Pike dispelling many a notion of a detour over Helvellyn. Eminently more inviting is the noble profile of Saint Sunday Crag beyond the tarn's outflow, and if considering an alternative route to Patterdale, this presents the easier option.

For the moment, however, descend to the foot of the tarn, one of the most popular picnic spots in the district. Certainly the mountain atmosphere here is strong, even if none show their finest faces. On leaving, the main route crosses the outflow to begin the descent to Patterdale by way of Grisedale's long but easy miles.

The head of Ullswater from Saint Sunday Crag

After passing the 'Brothers' Parting' stone, the path descends to Ruthwaite Lodge, a little below which is a fork. Either route will be enjoyed, the traditional one dropping down to the right to a footbridge over the beck and continuing without ado to the valley floor. The left branch crosses Ruthwaite Beck and remains on the north side of the valley, on the lower flanks of Striding Edge. It meets the Striding Edge path at its foot to join the main route (by now a farm road) in the valley bottom.

This narrow road drops down to the main road north of the village, though part-way down a gate on the right shows the way to a stile just above, from where an attractive finish through the trees of Glemara Park draws the day to a more suitable conclusion. Entry into Patterdale is by way of Mill Moss and the public conveniences.

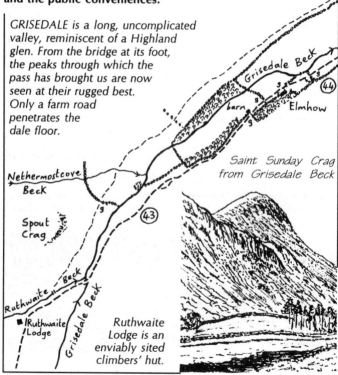

GRISEDALE is a long, uncomplicated valley, reminiscent of a Highland glen. From the bridge at its foot, the peaks through which the pass has brought us are now seen at their rugged best. Only a farm road penetrates the dale floor.

Grisedale Beck

barn

Elmhow

④④

Nethermostcove Beck

Saint Sunday Crag from Grisedale Beck

Spout Crag

g

④③

Ruthwaite Beck

Grisedale Beck

■ Ruthwaite Lodge

Ruthwaite Lodge is an enviably sited climbers' hut.

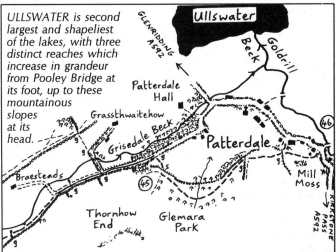

ULLSWATER is second largest and shapeliest of the lakes, with three distinct reaches which increase in grandeur from Pooley Bridge at its foot, up to these mountainous slopes at its head.

PATTERDALE is the undisputed capital of the Ullswater valley, standing at the head of the lake in the broad, green strath of the Goldrill Beck. It is not a large settlement, being its various components strung out along the A592. 'St. Patrick's Dale' is an extremely popular resort, but its lack of size has helped preserve it from the excessive commercialism of other central Lakeland villages. Boating and pony trekking are much enjoyed peaceful pastimes, while the slopes of the north-eastern Helvellyn range appeal to the ski-ing fraternity.

Although Patterdale is hemmed in by mountains, a motor road escapes north clinging to Ullswater's shore, and also south over the Kirkstone Pass. This connects with Windermere and Ambleside, and at the 1479ft summit it squeezes between fells a further thousand feet higher. On the very top is the Kirkstone Pass Inn, one of the highest in the country and formerly known as the Travellers' Rest.

Youth Hostel, Patterdale

STAGE 4

PATTERDALE
TO
SHAP

16 miles

*2700 feet
of ascent*

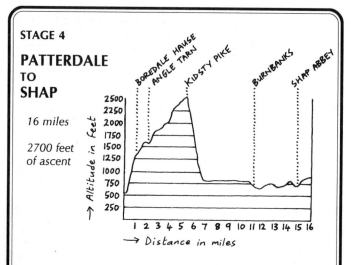

The enormous High Street ridge stands between us and faster progress towards the Yorkshire coast, and a promising forecast is especially appreciated for the morning of departure. While High Street is the parent fell of the group, an entire family of interlinking ridges spew forth from the windswept skyline that is the summit of the Coast to Coast Walk. The pass of Boredale Hause and the intricate curves of Angle Tarn break up the climb to the Straits of Rigginodale, where a clear day gives views far to the east, to Pennine country. From Kidsty Pike's precipitous crest the shore of Haweswater is soon alongside, and remains so until the final miles run through the verdant country of the river Lowther to Shap Abbey, well hidden from its village.

The nature of intervening valleys drilling deep into the hills makes this the only logical route, save for the enthusiast using it as a springboard to claim higher summits on and about the ridge. However, if an alternative is sought, usually due to poor weather, then a lower level, slightly longer walk follows Ullswater's shore to Howtown, there taking a bridleway onto Moor Divock to descend to the Lowther valley north of Bampton. This is no poor alternative, but actually a very enjoyable and relatively easy one.

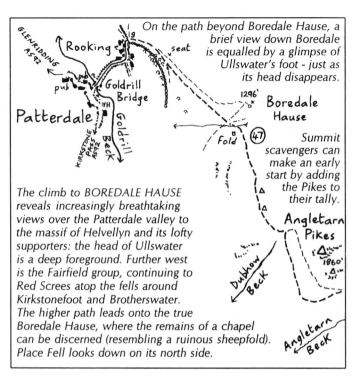

On the path beyond Boredale Hause, a brief view down Boredale is equalled by a glimpse of Ullswater's foot - just as its head disappears.

Summit scavengers can make an early start by adding the Pikes to their tally.

The climb to BOREDALE HAUSE reveals increasingly breathtaking views over the Patterdale valley to the massif of Helvellyn and its lofty supporters: the head of Ullswater is a deep foreground. Further west is the Fairfield group, continuing to Red Screes atop the fells around Kirkstonefoot and Brotherswater. The higher path leads onto the true Boredale Hause, where the remains of a chapel can be discerned (resembling a ruinous sheepfold). Place Fell looks down on its north side.

Leave the village by the side-road branching off just south of the **White Lion,** crossing Goldrill Beck and swinging round to the left to terminate in a corner by the houses of Rooking. A gate on the right gains the open fell, and a path slants away up to the right. At a fork below a seat keep to the lower path to rise effortlessly and quickly onto the broad, grassy saddle of Boredale Hause.

When the going eases at a cairn on a green plinth, cross the tiny beck above a sheepfold to a path winding up to the right. Tamer surrounds crowd in briefly before emergence above the head of Dubhow Beck, a classic moment as Brotherswater appears dramatically far below. A choice of higher or lower paths traverse the flank of Angletarn Pikes to the same goal, rounding a corner to find Angle Tarn outspread in front, and the great line of the High Street range marching across the skyline high above.

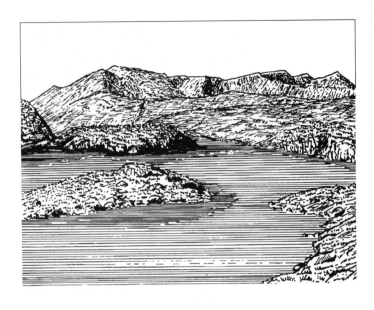

Looking back from Angle Tarn to the previous stage

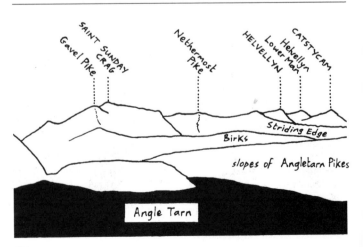

The path rounds the far side of the tarn and continues gently on up to a gate below Satura Crag. Be sure to cross the few yards to its cairned top to enjoy a super view down the length of Bannerdale before heading on through easy terrain below Rest Dodd. The whole of Hayeswater appears ahead beneath Thornthwaite Crag and Gray Crag, and an undulating trek ensues before crossing towards the dome of The Knott. Beyond the peaty environs of Sulphury Gill the path starts to climb again, merging with a path from Hartsop to reach a wall-corner just beneath the summit of The Knott. The great whaleback of High Street is just ahead now, and the path runs along the wallside to the airy saddle of the Straits of Riggindale.

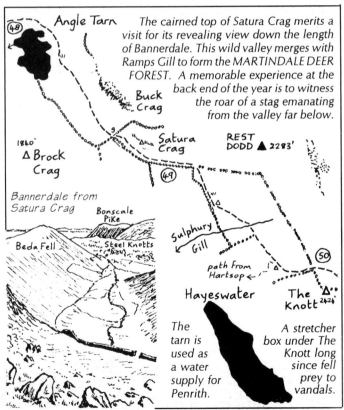

Angle Tarn

The cairned top of Satura Crag merits a visit for its revealing view down the length of Bannerdale. This wild valley merges with Ramps Gill to form the MARTINDALE DEER FOREST. A memorable experience at the back end of the year is to witness the roar of a stag emanating from the valley far below.

Buck Crag

Satura Crag

REST DODD ▲ 2283'

1840'
△ Brock Crag

Bannerdale from Satura Crag

Bonscale Pike

Beda Fell

Steel Knotts

Sulphury Gill

path from Hartsop ←

Hayeswater

The Knott 2424

The tarn is used as a water supply for Penrith.

A stretcher box under The Knott long since fell prey to vandals.

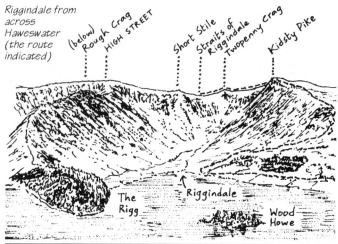

Riggindale from across Haweswater (the route indicated)

(below) Rough Crag · HIGH STREET · Short Stile · Straits of Riggindale · Twopenny Crag · Kidsty Pike

The Rigg · Riggindale · Wood Howe

KIDSTY PIKE has an impressive profile which masks the fact it is merely a minor upthrust on the shoulder of another mountain. Its spectacular drop into Riggindale is no sham, however, nor its position for appraising the craggy eastern face of High Street - or hoping to glimpse either a shy deer or a rather special bird.

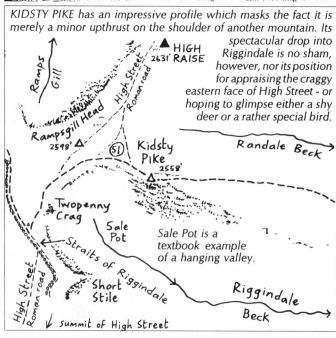

Ramps Gill

▲ HIGH RAISE 2631'

High Street Roman road

Rampsgill Head △ 2598'

Randale Beck

⑤① Kidsty Pike △ 2558'

Twopenny Crag

Sale Pot

Sale Pot is a textbook example of a hanging valley.

Straits of Riggindale

High Street Roman road

Short Stile

↓ summit of High Street

Riggindale Beck

The HIGH STREET ROMAN ROAD is a legendary highway linking the fort at Brougham, near Penrith, with Ambleside. It was their highest way in the country, reaching almost 2700 feet on the fell that now bears its name. The bare mountain top saw further action a couple of centuries ago, as a venue of horse races and sports linked with the Mardale shepherds' meet.

Summit cairn, Kidsty Pike

Double back sharply from this path junction to skirt round the rim of Riggindale to the waiting peak of Kidsty Pike, very much a place for an extended break. Far below at the foot of Riggindale, Haweswater shimmers, and when it's time to leave, a clear path quickly forms to pass a brace of shelters on a rash of stones on the declining east ridge. The path descends all the way to the lakeshore, taking the knobbly crest of Kidsty Howes in its stride. At the foot of the ridge join the lakeside path, turning left over a bridge on Randale Beck and along the length of Haweswater.

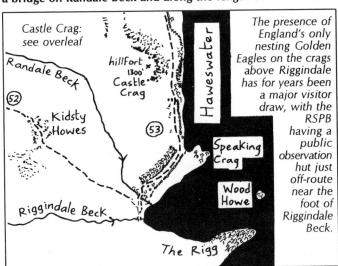

The presence of England's only nesting Golden Eagles on the crags above Riggindale has for years been a major visitor draw, with the RSPB having a public observation hut just off-route near the foot of Riggindale Beck.

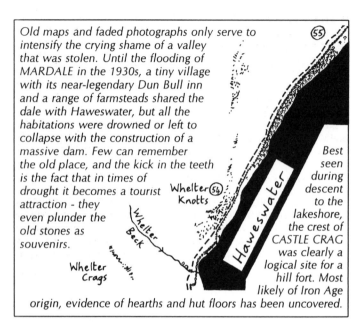

Old maps and faded photographs only serve to intensify the crying shame of a valley that was stolen. Until the flooding of MARDALE in the 1930s, a tiny village with its near-legendary Dun Bull inn and a range of farmsteads shared the dale with Haweswater, but all the habitations were drowned or left to collapse with the construction of a massive dam. Few can remember the old place, and the kick in the teeth is the fact that in times of drought it becomes a tourist attraction - they even plunder the old stones as souvenirs.

55

Whelter Knotts 54

Whelter Beck

Whelter Crags

Haweswater

Best seen during descent to the lakeshore, the crest of CASTLE CRAG was clearly a logical site for a hill fort. Most likely of Iron Age origin, evidence of hearths and hut floors has been uncovered.

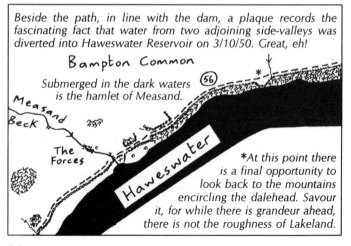

Beside the path, in line with the dam, a plaque records the fascinating fact that water from two adjoining side-valleys was diverted into Haweswater Reservoir on 3/10/50. Great, eh!

Bampton Common

Submerged in the dark waters is the hamlet of Measand.

56

Measand Beck

The Forces

Haweswater

*At this point there is a final opportunity to look back to the mountains encircling the dalehead. Savour it, for while there is grandeur ahead, there is not the roughness of Lakeland.

The route runs along the entire length of the reservoir on a clear path throughout, always with a wall or fence keeping us from polluting the water. In its later stages the way becomes a broad track to drop to a stile by a gate, then descends through trees to a rough road down to the cottages at Burnbanks. Go left along the road out of the hamlet, but within a minute locate a gateway on the right, from where a path runs through delightful woodland to where Naddle Bridge strides over Haweswater Beck. Cross the road to descend to more woodland, but at once also cross the main beck by a parallel, defunct stone-arched bridge, and inflowing Naddle Beck by a footbridge - an interesting corner!

Head downstream in the lovely environs of the beck, passing Thornthwaite Force and the shapely packhorse bridge of Park Bridge in quick succession. After a brief break from the beck, a wide track forms to soon rise above a wooded bank to cross a side-stream to a stile. Here forsake the valley of Haweswater Beck by following the fence-side up to the barns of High Park, then steer left across the field towards a stile in a fence opposite.

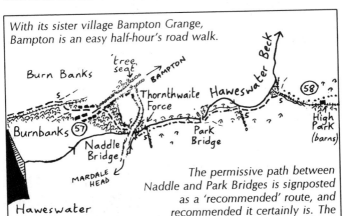

With its sister village Bampton Grange, Bampton is an easy half-hour's road walk.

Burn Banks

'tree seat'

BAMPTON

Thornthwaite Force

Haweswater Beck

58

Burnbanks 57

Naddle Bridge

MARDALE HEAD

Park Bridge

High Park (barns)

Haweswater

The permissive path between Naddle and Park Bridges is signposted as a 'recommended' route, and recommended it certainly is. The beckside walk is in itself a wooded delight, with the addition of effervescent Thornthwaite Force adding greatly to its charms.

BURNBANKS is composed of a few simple dwellings built for the reservoir employees. Two rather quaint MCWW (Manchester Corporation Water Works) signposts point the way towards a 'fellside track' - the one we came down upon.

55

SHAP ABBEY is the only abbey in old Westmorland, and is a rarity also in its proximity to the high mountains. Founded around the end of the 12th century, it housed White Canons belonging to the Premonstratensian order (see also Easby, near Richmond). The tower presides over otherwise low-lying ruins, much of the stone having found its way into the adjoining farm. Its setting, as ever, is idyllic, and the cost to savour it? Nothing at all.

Shap Abbey

The **RIVER LOWTHER** flows for sixteen miles from the dam of Wet Sleddale Reservoir to its entry into the Eamont near Penrith. Its grassy banks are emphatically free of man's interference, the only settlement to take advantage being Bampton Grange, which can hardly be regarded as a blemish.

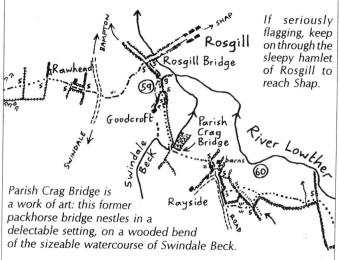

If seriously flagging, keep on through the sleepy hamlet of Rosgill to reach Shap.

Parish Crag Bridge is a work of art: this former packhorse bridge nestles in a delectable setting, on a wooded bend of the sizeable watercourse of Swindale Beck.

*Rest on this stile at the field-top to look back at the northern High Street ridge, with Kidsty Pike re-appearing in its inimitable way.

56

The faint path runs a direct course through a couple more fields to the attractive white-walled Rawhead, following its drive out onto an open road. Cross straight over on a path that bears left over gorse-filled moorland to descend to another road at Rosgill Bridge. Barely impinging on the tarmac, turn sharp right onto a drive upstream by the river Lowther. At the next gate/stile forsake the drive and keep left with a wall, passing below the farm of Goodcroft and alongside a fence to discover Parish Crag Bridge on Swindale Beck. Up the bank behind, head up the field towards a barn on the skyline, passing through an enclosure occupied by a motley assortment of barns to meet a narrow road on a corner.

Turn up the road (passing the stile of an alternative path - see map) until the accompanying wall breaks off left, then do likewise by aiming across to a stile beyond marshy ground. Follow the wall away to a corner, from where cross a large field: on the brow the tower of Shap Abbey appears. Slant down to a stile in the far corner, and a final field is crossed to meet the Lowther just before the abbey. Curve right above the bank to a stile, dropping to the abbey's green access track. On the left Abbey Bridge leads into the car park and the road climbing away, but the abbey ruins can first be inspected. Back at Abbey Bridge, the concrete road climbs steeply (cruelly so, at this stage) through a field. The way becomes a narrow lane to meet another road running along to enter Shap. An alternative finish uses a stile left of the cattle-grid to run parallel to the road (see map). Turn right for the centre.

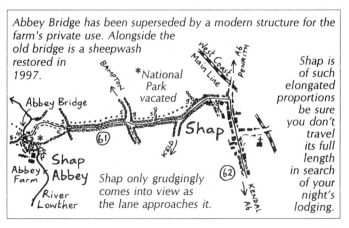

Abbey Bridge has been superseded by a modern structure for the farm's private use. Alongside the old bridge is a sheepwash restored in 1997.

*National Park vacated

Shap is of such elongated proportions be sure you don't travel its full length in search of your night's lodging.

Shap only grudgingly comes into view as the lane approaches it.

57

STAGE 5

SHAP TO KIRKBY STEPHEN

21 miles *1600 feet of ascent*

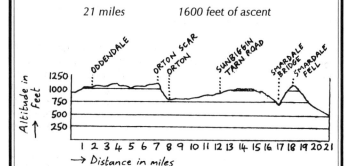

A marvellous range of scenery is matched by a remarkable concentration of features deeply rooted in history during this long but easy walk. This crossing of the Westmorland plateau is dominated by limestone underfoot and distant views of rolling hills: back to Lakeland, south to the Howgill Fells, and east to the Pennines. The only village encountered is Orton, a pleasant interlude between the stone circles, prehistoric settlements and a large tarn that form integral parts of this grand march.

There is little scope for finding a shorter way, but certainly alternatives exist, either southerly on the Roman road to Orton and then through the upper Lune Valley to Newbiggin on Lune and perhaps Ravenstonedale; or northerly to Crosby Ravensworth, Bank Moor, Little Asby, Potts Valley and Crosby Garrett.

Shap is hardly jigsaw material, but it can boast this fine building. Three hundred years old, it stands midway along the main street (west side).

Market Hall, Shap

Leave the main street by suburban Moss Grove opposite the *Kings Arms*, soon turning right on a road that becomes a rough track climbing to a bridge over the railway line. Continuing between hedgerows, bear right at a fork beyond a barn, our green way soon emerging into a field. With the outline of a motorway footbridge ahead, three fields are crossed to earn the satisfaction of crossing the M6, a landmark event.

More important is the fact that Kirkby Stephen is 20 miles distant, so press on by turning right on the other side. Beyond a wall-end the thin path slants up through boulders and hawthorn to a brow, below which is the Hardendale road alongside the restored house at The Nab. Cross over and bear right on a gentle green way to a wall-corner, rising left slightly to approach Hardendale Quarry. Beyond a fence, follow the wall and a stile on the right leads to a pair of step-flights flanking the quarry road.

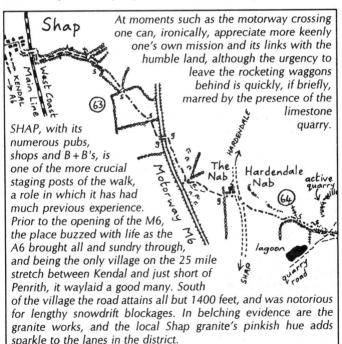

At moments such as the motorway crossing one can, ironically, appreciate more keenly one's own mission and its links with the humble land, although the urgency to leave the rocketing waggons behind is quickly, if briefly, marred by the presence of the limestone quarry.

SHAP, with its numerous pubs, shops and B + B's, is one of the more crucial staging posts of the walk, a role in which it has had much previous experience. Prior to the opening of the M6, the place buzzed with life as the A6 brought all and sundry through, and being the only village on the 25 mile stretch between Kendal and just short of Penrith, it waylaid a good many. South of the village the road attains all but 1400 feet, and was notorious for lengthy snowdrift blockages. In belching evidence are the granite works, and the local Shap granite's pinkish hue adds sparkle to the lanes in the district.

On the other side a dusty road heads away to Oddendale, hidden in trees. At the entrance keep outside its confines on a similarly broad track rising onto the grassy moor. Easily missed is Oddendale Stone Circle across to the right, as the broad green track runs on to a large, walled enclosure. Keeping left of it a slight green way advances on, with Crosby Ravensworth Fell outspread ahead. At a slight depression, bear down to the left past a crumbling bield (sheep shelter) to the corner of a plantation, from where a slim path heads up the slope beyond. The distinct course of a Roman road is crossed to rise to a tumulus marked by a signpost.

Head on through a small limestone pavement to drop to an immense Shap granite boulder (an erratic, for it rests on limestone). The clear path now descends to cross the embryo Lyvennet and rises improvingly to a wall corner, with the Black Dub monument a little upstream (no right of way).

> HERE AT BLACK DUB
> THE SOURCE OF THE LIVENNET
> KING CHARLES THE II
> REGALED HIS ARMY
> AND DRANK OF THE WATER
> ON HIS MARCH FROM SCOTLAND
> AUGUST 8 1651

The Monument
at Black Dub
(and inscription)

60

Hardendale
Quarry

quarry
extension

SHAP

Oddendale

The farming hamlet of Oddendale enjoys an enviable seclusion from the outside world.

ROUTE NOTE: From mile 66 to 69 the route is on permissive paths only: please adhere strictly to the recommended route.

(65)

Oddendale
Stone
Circle

cairn on
tumulus

The Roman road over Crosby Ravensworth Fell was their route between forts at Low Borrow Bridge in the Lune Gorge, and Kirkby Thore, in Eden Vale.

ODDENDALE STONE CIRCLE
is easily located, being sited just beyond a minor outbreak of limestone. The circle, however, is constructed of the distinctive Shap granite boulders. A compact inner kerb sits inside a near-30 yards wide outer ring. It makes a grand viewpoint for Lakeland's fells.

Seal
Howe
x
1161'

bield

(66)

The tumulus on the brow above the Roman road is pinpointed by a 'Ministry of Works' sign that would appear little less ancient than the burial cairn itself.

Roman road

1171'
x Tumulus
shelter

boulder

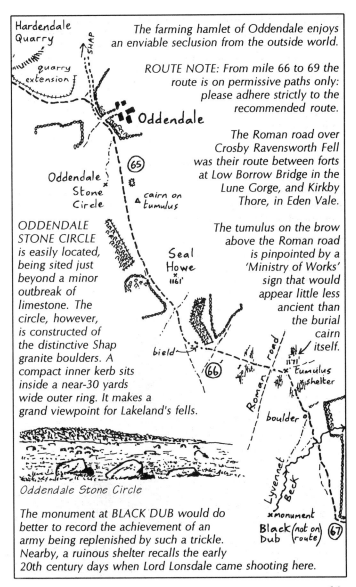

Oddendale Stone Circle

Lyvennet Beck

The monument at BLACK DUB would do better to record the achievement of an army being replenished by such a trickle. Nearby, a ruinous shelter recalls the early 20th century days when Lord Lonsdale came shooting here.

x monument
Black (not on
Dub   route)

(67)

61

At the corner the wall is followed away, a grand grassy path descending through the heather, past Robin Hood's Grave and then climbing away. When the wall parts company head over the brow, and with an old quarry as a target, drop to a stile in a fence lining the moorland road from Orton to Crosby Ravensworth. Slanting right, cross over to a slender trod heading into the recess of a dry valley below a plantation. The thin path is followed up to its demise at the meeting of the earlier road with the B6260 to Appleby, a superb moment with the Howgill Fells magnificent beyond the patchwork pastures of the upper Lune Valley.

Crossing the cattle-grid the route heads down into Orton, either directly by road, or by a more leisurely and hugely attractive bridleway. Just across the grid drop left to a gate, which sees a green way curve down to Broadfell Farm. *NB: if omitting Orton, slant left of the farm to join its drive, following it out to a road. Go left, passing two farms on sharp bends. Just after the second a path branches left to cross to a stile onto Knott Lane, and the main route.* At Broadfell, cross the yard between the buildings, and slant down to the field-corner below. Here a track runs parallel with a stream. On crossing the tiny watercourse to a gate into a meadow, remain with the stream, to become enclosed well before emerging into a quiet corner of the village. Bear right, right again then left on the main road into the village centre.

Limekiln, Orton Scar

Robin Hood's Grave

The clearly discernible line of an ancient dyke marks the upper limit of a serene parkland reaching down to Crosby Ravensworth.

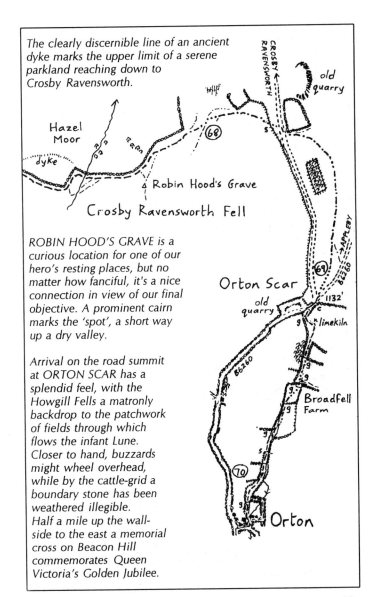

Hazel Moor

dyke

Robin Hood's Grave

Crosby Ravensworth Fell

CROSBY RAVENSWORTH

old quarry

68

Orton Scar

old quarry

APPLEBY B6260

69

1132'

limekiln

B6260

Broadfell Farm

70

Orton

ROBIN HOOD'S GRAVE is a curious location for one of our hero's resting places, but no matter how fanciful, it's a nice connection in view of our final objective. A prominent cairn marks the 'spot', a short way up a dry valley.

Arrival on the road summit at ORTON SCAR has a splendid feel, with the Howgill Fells a matronly backdrop to the patchwork of fields through which flows the infant Lune. Closer to hand, buzzards might wheel overhead, while by the cattle-grid a boundary stone has been weathered illegible. Half a mile up the wall-side to the east a memorial cross on Beacon Hill commemorates Queen Victoria's Golden Jubilee.

At Orton

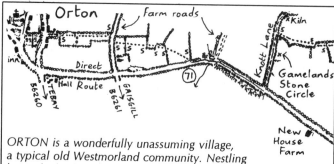

ORTON is a wonderfully unassuming village,
a typical old Westmorland community. Nestling
beneath the limestone watershed, it overlooks the upper Lune
Valley, and the number of roads and lanes homing in suggests a
greater importance in days gone by. Old houses and chapels and
a gurgling roadside stream give the village centre great charm,
while the parish church, spanning eight centuries, watches over
things from a knoll. Perhaps of greater immediate interest are the
more obvious attractions of pub, shop and tearooms.

The map shows two routes out of Orton, re-uniting before Knott Lane. The direct route continues on the road past the *George Hotel*, turning left at the edge of the village along the Raisbeck road, for a mile as far as unsurfaced Knott Lane on the left. The more time-consuming field path departs across the main road from the square, first stage being an urban-type path past playing fields to another stream and a back road. A snicket between houses opposite sends the way along a field-side to join a narrow back lane. A few yards right another stile sees the invisible path through several fields, slanting right to join the direct route: Knott Lane is a quarter-mile further, on the left.

Part way up Knott Lane, look over the wall on the right to see Gamelands Stone Circle. Just past it, take a stile on the right. The addition of stiles to the many gates of this bridleway has made life much easier. Head away to a stile in a kink of the wall ahead, then simply forge straight on through a series of stiles, passing in front of a barn. Two final, larger pastures are crossed to emerge onto Sunbiggin Lane, just in front of Acres Farm. Turn left on this cul-de-sac lane to the farming hamlet of Sunbiggin, and keep right on the road to its demise, where a green lane takes up the running.

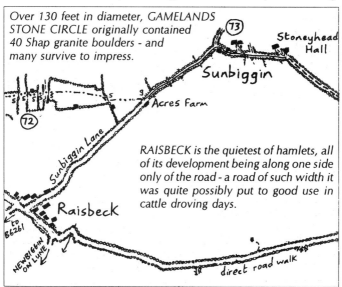

Over 130 feet in diameter, GAMELANDS STONE CIRCLE originally contained 40 Shap granite boulders - and many survive to impress.

73

Stoneyhead Hall

Sunbiggin

Acres Farm

72

Sunbiggin Lane

RAISBECK is the quietest of hamlets, all of its development being along one side only of the road - a road of such width it was quite possibly put to good use in cattle droving days.

Raisbeck

to B6261

NEWBIGGIN ON LUNE

direct road walk

The impending proximity of Sunbiggin Tarn is quite likely to be ascertained well in advance, due to the presence of breeding gulls. On the direct path, it comes into view midway between the stile and the Asby road. Tarn Moor also enjoys a magnificent prospect of the Howgill Fells.

Spear Pots is a juicy mire, haunt of birds and ringed with hides.

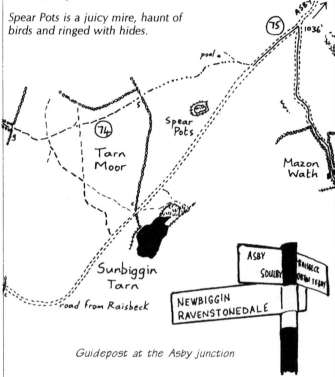

Guidepost at the Asby junction

SUNBIGGIN TARN is a refreshing sight in these expansive limestone uplands, though as it is graded a *Site of Special Scientific Interest*, with no rights of way, the walk no longer visits the shoreline, as it once did. The option for a closer look at Sunbiggin Tarn turns right at the first crossroads of tracks on Tarn Moor. Keep left at an early fork then right at another path crossroads to drop down onto the open road opposite the tarn.

The pleasant green lane from Sunbiggin emerges onto Tarn Moor. Heading away to a crossroads in a hollow, a choice of routes awaits. The direct route omits a detour to Sunbiggin Tarn: keep straight on, rising to another junction. While a track runs across the route, the way forges on yet again, now as a slimmer green path through the heather. Though diminishing somewhat, it runs meekly on to reach a stile in a boundary wall. Largely grassy moorland now replaces heather, and an 'invisible' path crosses this easy terrain, contouring well above the hollow of Spear Pots to work round to the unfenced road seen ahead.

Turn left along the broad verge as far as a junction, then double back to the right (signposted Newbiggin and Ravenstonedale) to trace a similar road to the farm of Mazon Wath. Continuing over a cattle-grid the road quickly breaks free again and rises over the moor to cross another cattle-grid. This time, turn left with the wall skirting Ewefell Mire to a gate at the far end. The track continues away under Great Ewe Fell, passing an advertisement for Bents Farm, rather handy if you can't go a step further.

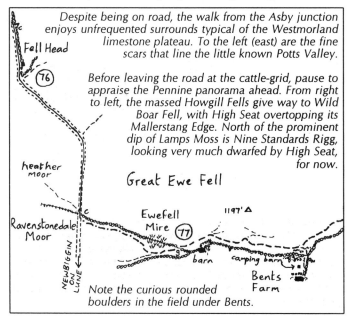

Despite being on road, the walk from the Asby junction enjoys unfrequented surrounds typical of the Westmorland limestone plateau. To the left (east) are the fine scars that line the little known Potts Valley.

Fell Head

76

Before leaving the road at the cattle-grid, pause to appraise the Pennine panorama ahead. From right to left, the massed Howgill Fells give way to Wild Boar Fell, with High Seat overtopping its Mallerstang Edge. North of the prominent dip of Lamps Moss is Nine Standards Rigg, looking very much dwarfed by High Seat, for now.

heather moor

Great Ewe Fell

Ravenstonedale Moor

NEWBIGGIN ON LUNE

Ewefell Mire 77

1197' △

barn

camping barn

Bents Farm

Note the curious rounded boulders in the field under Bents.

67

The expanse of Crosby Garrett Fell is an archaeologists' paradise, and the largest of its prehistoric field systems is SEVERALS village settlement. Better appraised in aerial pictures is this labyrinth of grassy mounds that formed hut enclosures at the centre of converging field boundaries. The path has been re-routed to halt its march through the middle.

Crosby
Garrett
Fell

As well as the impressive viaduct, look for the 'on-site' quarry in this fascinating side-valley of SMARDALE.

A nature reserve now exists here.

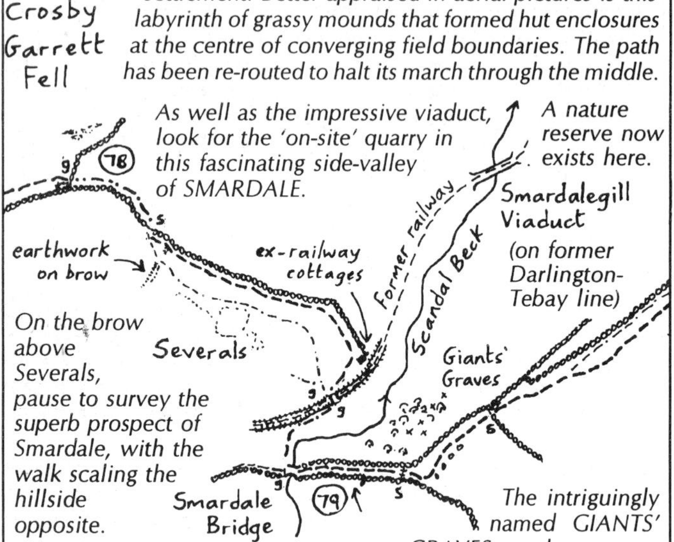

Smardalegill Viaduct

(on former Darlington-Tebay line)

earthwork on brow

ex-railway cottages

former railway

Scandal Beck

Severals

Giants' Graves

On the brow above Severals, pause to survey the superb prospect of Smardale, with the walk scaling the hillside opposite.

Smardale Bridge

The intriguingly named GIANTS' GRAVES are shown more descriptively on maps as 'pillow mounds', and are of uncertain origin. It is possible they were constructed as rabbit warrens, some time after their introduction into Britain by the Normans.

Public paths at either end of Smardale Bridge lead through a 16th century deer park to Ravenstonedale, a lovely village no matter how tired one might be.

Smardale Bridge

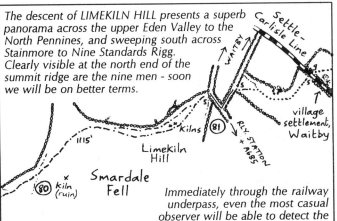

The descent of LIMEKILN HILL presents a superb panorama across the upper Eden Valley to the North Pennines, and sweeping south across Stainmore to Nine Standards Rigg. Clearly visible at the north end of the summit ridge are the nine men - soon we will be on better terms.

Immediately through the railway underpass, even the most casual observer will be able to detect the presence of WAITBY village settlement. Just to the right are the distinct outlines of a rectangular earthwork with an arrangement of internal enclosures, not all destroyed by the rail embankment.

The SETTLE-CARLISLE RAILWAY is probably the most famous line in the country, thanks largely to the monumental campaign that culminated in its salvation in 1989. As we encounter it, it has just broken free of the enveloping Pennines, and is set for a triumphant journey through the Eden Valley.

The green track continues along the wallside beyond Bents to the next gate in the wall. From it follow a wall away to a stile, then instead of taking the old path slanting away, remain with the wall on a permissive path. It rises to the brow then descends with the wall, with Severals village settlement just to the right. Swing right on approaching derelict cottages to reach a bridge over a former railway line. Go right a short way to descend to the waiting Smardale Bridge.

Across it a superb old green road breasts the steep slope, which soon relents to enjoy a gentle traverse of the wide open spaces of Smardale Fell. At the end it descends above two old limekilns to a stile onto a back lane. Follow it right on its central green strip just as far as a junction, then go left to another stile on the right. Wind around a large field to a railway underpass ahead, from which bear gently right to locate a stile by the far corner.

Just into the field is the long-awaited first glimpse of Kirkby Stephen - a long day is drawing to a close! Slanting down a small field, the head of a dry hollow is rounded as the way slants left, down through a large pasture to a stile at the bottom by a few trees. Descend past an island barn to an abandoned double railway underpass to enter the yard of Green Riggs Farm.

The way is clearly marked through two gates on the right and then out along the farm road all the way to Kirkby Stephen, passing the flat-topped site of Croglam Castle just up to the right. The back lane - not a classic entry to the town - can be followed as far as desired in order to avoid the main road, though it can be joined much earlier. A fitting way is to keep on as far as the rear of the *Pennine Hotel*, just past which an alleyway leads into the town centre opposite the Market Place - the point at which it will be left.

KIRKBY STEPHEN is small, tiny even as towns go, but in the heart of a vast rural area its importance is far greater. Its market charter was granted in 1361, and today the Market Place remains the heart of things. Numerous characterful buildings are grouped around, with the church of St. Stephen, dating in parts from the mid-13th century, stood behind the cloisters of 1810. Inside, the Wharton and Musgrave chapels have effigies of members of these historically important local families. Pride of place goes to the Loki Stone, part of a 1000 year old Norse cross featuring a bound devil: Loki was a Viking god, and the carving is thought to symbolise Christianity overcoming paganism.

Alongside the church are the old parsonage dating from 1677, and the old grammar school founded by Thomas Wharton in 1566 and in use as such for almost 400 years. Across the main road is an old knitting gallery in what is known as the Shambles. Like Shap before it, Kirkby Stephen clings to its main road and displays little width. A useful feature is the welcoming number of cafes to complement the handful of pubs.

*Old roadsign,
Kirkby Stephen*

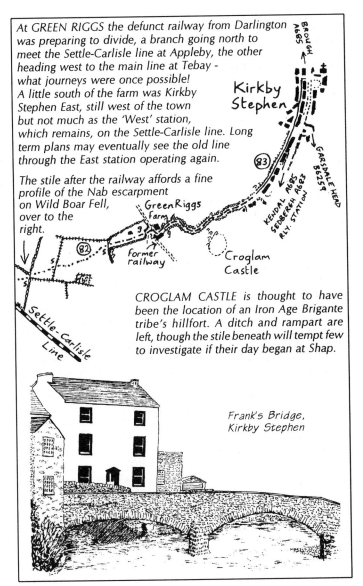

At GREEN RIGGS the defunct railway from Darlington was preparing to divide, a branch going north to meet the Settle-Carlisle line at Appleby, the other heading west to the main line at Tebay - what journeys were once possible! A little south of the farm was Kirkby Stephen East, still west of the town but not much as the 'West' station, which remains, on the Settle-Carlisle line. Long term plans may eventually see the old line through the East station operating again.

The stile after the railway affords a fine profile of the Nab escarpment on Wild Boar Fell, over to the right.

CROGLAM CASTLE is thought to have been the location of an Iron Age Brigante tribe's hillfort. A ditch and rampart are left, though the stile beneath will tempt few to investigate if their day began at Shap.

Frank's Bridge, Kirkby Stephen

STAGE 6

KIRKBY STEPHEN
TO
KELD

12 miles

*1900 feet
of ascent*

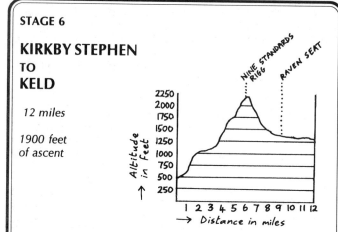

This is the crossing of the Pennine watershed, the backbone of England. Nine Standards Rigg is also a very suitable place to celebrate such an occasion, being an outstanding viewpoint and endowed with various adornments of which the famous Nine Standards are pre-eminent. The ascent is remarkably easy, largely on grass verges or green trackways: only the upper limits remind you that a mountain has been climbed. The long descent to the headwaters of the Swale is true Pennine in character, a wild country that is changed little by the arrival in Whitsundale's side-valley, and only on nearing Keld is there a warmer feel.

As the route over Nine Standards Rigg is still not a right of way, the authorities have negotiated permissive routes based on seasons of the year. This is principally to allow the ground to recover from increasing erosion. The two main routes diverge after leaving the summit, and are clearly identified both in the text and on the maps. A third, safer option was recommended in the first edition of this guide. It has now been taken up as the 'official' line in poor weather or in winter, and this too is clearly described. All variants re-unite before reaching Raven Seat.

As this is not the first attempt at varying the route over the fell, please heed any further changes, should they appear.

Leave the Market Place outside the church by the short lane past the toilets, descending Stoneshot and cutting down a snicket to cross the Eden at Frank's Bridge. Turn right with the river only as far as a bend, and from the kissing-gate take a surfaced wallside path away from the river. It runs on to join a back lane in Hartley.

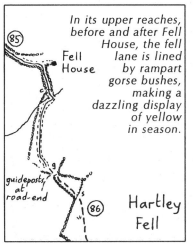

In its upper reaches, before and after Fell House, the fell lane is lined by rampant gorse bushes, making a dazzling display of yellow in season.

Go right for just 75 yards, locating a path down to a little footbridge. Continue right along a parallel road behind, which quickly swings left to climb past the entrance to the vast Hartley Quarry. Sanity returns as the lane eventually levels out to approach the isolated farm of Fell House. It runs on still further to end at a fork, where the left branch rises through a gate onto Hartley Fell.

73

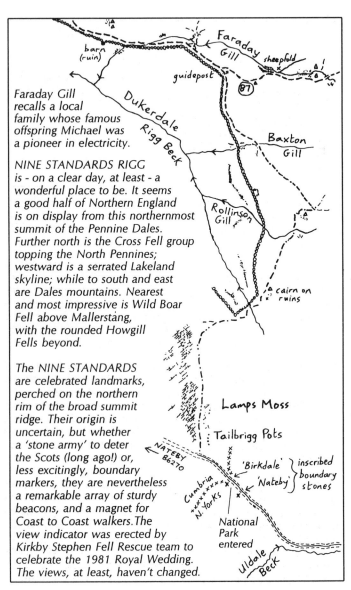

Faraday Gill recalls a local family whose famous offspring Michael was a pioneer in electricity.

NINE STANDARDS RIGG is - on a clear day, at least - a wonderful place to be. It seems a good half of Northern England is on display from this northernmost summit of the Pennine Dales. Further north is the Cross Fell group topping the North Pennines; westward is a serrated Lakeland skyline; while to south and east are Dales mountains. Nearest and most impressive is Wild Boar Fell above Mallerstang, with the rounded Howgill Fells beyond.

The NINE STANDARDS are celebrated landmarks, perched on the northern rim of the broad summit ridge. Their origin is uncertain, but whether a 'stone army' to deter the Scots (long ago!) or, less excitingly, boundary markers, they are nevertheless a remarkable array of sturdy beacons, and a magnet for Coast to Coast walkers. The view indicator was erected by Kirkby Stephen Fell Rescue team to celebrate the 1981 Royal Wedding. The views, at least, haven't changed.

74

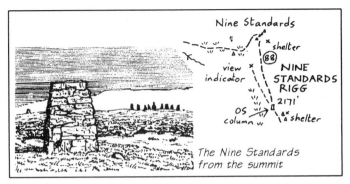

The Nine Standards
from the summit

With the Nine Standards seen intermittently ahead, the broad track soon rises by a wall. As the going eases, wall and track slant right, and at a guidepost the route departs from the public bridleway. Here departs the first seasonal variation.

•<u>DECEMBER-APRIL</u> Remain on the wallside, a level grassy march before leaving the wall to rise gently over the fell. Beyond Baxton Gill it is a thinner path leading to a junction, with the landmark cairn of Jack Standards on the skyline in front. At this junction turn sharp right, descending 100 yards to a ruinous shelter-cairn above a rash of stones. This is the highest point of the climb: note the distinct limestone boundary on Lamps Moss below.

A thin path zigzags down the bank, bearing left over a stream and on towards the wall enclosing the head of Dukerdale. Cross the stream, but up the other side bear left as the wall turns right. An intermittent green way runs by the limestone pavement to meet the unfenced B6270 at its summit. Go left, quickly passing myriad boundary signs. Maintaining the theme, a pair of more traditional parish boundary stones are passed as the road angles down for a long descent into the headwaters of the Swale.

•<u>MAY-NOVEMBER</u> The guidepost sends a similarly distinct green track directly up the fell. This soon resumes shadowing Faraday Gill, rising above a modest ravine to a brace of cairns framing the impending Standards. Over less comfortable terrain the path treads a section of crazy paving amongst peat groughs before gaining the beacons. Visible to the south is the Ordnance column on the summit of the fell, and a path runs easily thereto, a deviation taking in the prominent view indicator en route.

•**MAY-NOVEMBER** The walk continues south past a pair of cairns and a shelter, down to the peaty saddle before White Mossy Hill. Across this enclave of groughs is the second seasonal variation.

•**AUGUST-NOVEMBER** Turn sharp left down a broad swathe of glutinous path, descending ever gently towards the lovely side-valley of Whitsundale. Marker posts highlight the peaty route.

•**MAY-JULY** Keep straight on and up a minor rise to White Mossy Hill, its plain summit marked only by a couple of recumbent stones. The path continues a gradual, peaty descent towards Swaledale, with Birkdale Tarn ahead and the heights of Rogan's Seat and Great Shunner Fell hemming in the upper dale. Beyond a shelter, a prominent 8ft pillar on the boulders of Millstones makes an obvious halting place before the path moves pleasantly on down to intercept a shooters' track. Its hard surface is followed left only as far as the cabin it serves.

•**DECEMBER-APRIL** The road is followed for a mile and a half through bleak, rolling moorland, gently declining as it goes. It is left on a bend when a lone guidepost sends a path left over a little brow to almost at once join a shooters' track leaving the road. Go left on this to its demise at a shooting cabin.

The pillar on Millstones, looking to High Pike Hill

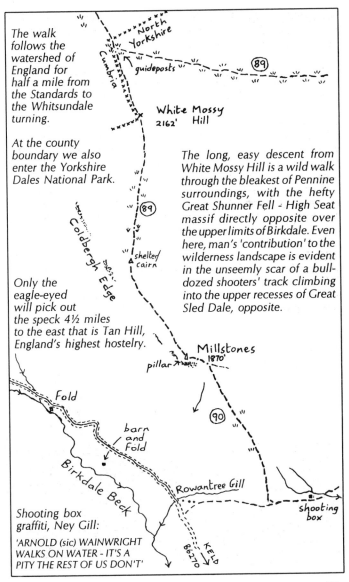

The walk follows the watershed of England for half a mile from the Standards to the Whitsundale turning.

At the county boundary we also enter the Yorkshire Dales National Park.

Only the eagle-eyed will pick out the speck 4½ miles to the east that is Tan Hill, England's highest hostelry.

North Yorkshire

Cumbria

guideposts

89

White Mossy Hill
2162'

89

shelter/cairn

Coldbergh Edge

The long, easy descent from White Mossy Hill is a wild walk through the bleakest of Pennine surroundings, with the hefty Great Shunner Fell – High Seat massif directly opposite over the upper limits of Birkdale. Even here, man's 'contribution' to the wilderness landscape is evident in the unseemly scar of a bulldozed shooters' track climbing into the upper recesses of Great Sled Dale, opposite.

Millstones
1870'

pillar

90

Fold

barn and Fold

Birkdale Beck

Rowantree Gill

KELD
B6270

shooting box

Shooting box graffiti, Ney Gill:

'ARNOLD (sic) WAINWRIGHT WALKS ON WATER - IT'S A PITY THE REST OF US DON'T'

•AUGUST-NOVEMBER Just short of Whitsundale Beck the path is ushered right, along the valley side. Keeping above the beck, the clear path runs a generally pleasant course down this once unfrequented dale. Eventually entering a tract of regenerating heather moorland, the path descends and runs along to a wall, which deflects it right, over a low brow to join the footpath alongside Ney Gill. Go left with the stream, quickly crossing it and rising to follow the wall around to drop down onto the cul-de-sac road into Raven Seat.

• DECEMBER-JULY From the hut a more accommodating foot-path takes over. The stream of Ney Gill provides company, and is briefly crossed at one point as a fence and old wall nudge us off course. When a wall crosses the beck do likewise, rising to follow the wall around to drop down onto the cul-de-sac road into Raven Seat.

• ALL 3 RE-UNITED Cross the cattle-grid into the farming hamlet, and over the shapely bridge turn immediately up towards the house on the right. In its yard a gate on the right sets a course that runs along the opposite bank, parallel with Whitsundale Beck.

At Raven Seat

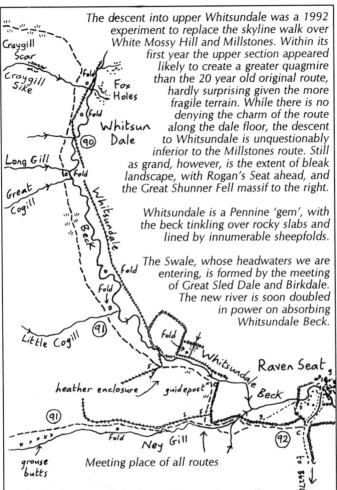

The descent into upper Whitsundale was a 1992 experiment to replace the skyline walk over White Mossy Hill and Millstones. Within its first year the upper section appeared likely to create a greater quagmire than the 20 year old original route, hardly surprising given the more fragile terrain. While there is no denying the charm of the route along the dale floor, the descent to Whitsundale is unquestionably inferior to the Millstones route. Still as grand, however, is the extent of bleak landscape, with Rogan's Seat ahead, and the Great Shunner Fell massif to the right.

Whitsundale is a Pennine 'gem', with the beck tinkling over rocky slabs and lined by innumerable sheepfolds.

The Swale, whose headwaters we are entering, is formed by the meeting of Great Sled Dale and Birkdale. The new river is soon doubled in power on absorbing Whitsundale Beck.

Map labels: Craygill Scar · Craygill Sike · Fox Holes · Whitsun Dale · (90) · Long Gill · Great Cogill · Whitsundale Beck · fold · Little Cogill · (91) · fold · Whitsundale · Raven Seat · Beck · heather enclosure · guidepost · (91) · Fold · Ney Gill · Meeting place of all routes · (92) · grouse butts · to B6270

In the final section to the Raven Seat road, a small gate on the brow on the left (see map) indicates a variation approach to the farm, which descends to a ladder-stile by the beck and then follows it around to the bridge at the road-end. This is in fact the true right of way, though it has largely been usurped by the path remaining on the moor to the cattle-grid.

From a gate just above an attractive waterfall climb half-left to a barn, thence continuing on a higher level through the pastures above the superb and unexpected scenery of How Edge Scars and Oven Mouth. Beyond a gate in a fence the path forks: take the right one to pass along the base of a large crumbling enclosure. Continue on the level trod beyond, bearing left above the barns of Smithy Holme to arrive at a gate in the corner. A good track now drops past a farm and down towards the Kirkby Stephen-Keld road at Low Bridge.

After a gate before the final drop however, go left along the top of a crumbled wall, to commence a level march along the unseen crest of the wooded top of Cotterby Scar. Wainwath Force is seen below as the path turns to descend to the Tan Hill road, on a bend just above its junction with the valley road. Go down it to the bridge over the Swale and turn left for Keld, on what remains one of the longest quarter-miles in the North.

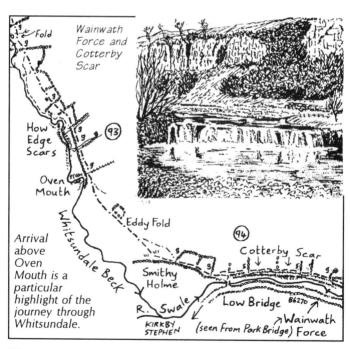

Wainwath Force and Cotterby Scar

How Edge Scars

93

Oven Mouth

Whitsundale Beck

Eddy Fold

94

Cotterby Scar

Smithy Holme

R. Swale

Low Bridge B6270

KIRKBY STEPHEN

(seen from Park Bridge)

Wainwath Force

Arrival above Oven Mouth is a particular highlight of the journey through Whitsundale.

Kisdon Force, Keld

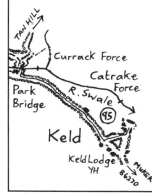

KELD is the first outpost of any size in Swaledale, and is a welcoming apparition in our descent from the high country. The heart of this old Norse settlement is found grouped around a sloping square, below the main road but high above the Swale. Its hostelry the 'Cat Hole Inn' long since called time, though at this meeting place of Coast to Coast Walk and Pennine Way, it would, ironically, more than likely pay its way today. Unchanged, however, are the waterfalls, and these are what makes Keld special.

STAGE 7

KELD TO REETH

11 miles

*1800 feet
of ascent*

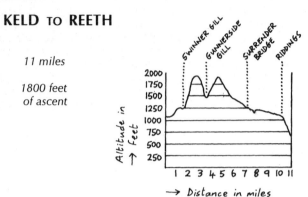

This direct march over the moors is short but time-consuming, certainly if taking any interest in the wealth of remains of a once-thriving lead industry. In the recesses of Swinner Gill, Gunnerside Gill and Hard Level Gill are the ruins of smelting mills and associated workings, while the intervening moortops still sport their vast tracts of mining debris. It's not all savage industrial wilderness however, for charming deep-cut gills and purple heather moors are interspersed, and in the latter stages the mining scenes give way entirely to the softer surrounds of Swaledale at its brilliant best.

The only unfortunate aspect of this route is that it does not more satisfyingly combine moorland with the valley scenery, and for this reason many Coast to Coasters choose to take the valley option, which more than does justice to the beautiful, rushing Swale. This runs an entirely different route to the main one, on a parallel course shadowing the Swale downstream. Riverside paths for the most part ensure the Swale is rarely forsaken, and even the innumerable stiles fail to compensate for the ups and downs of the moorland route. Last but not least, this enticing alternative has one - or rather several - further advantages, namely a variety of refreshment venues throughout its length.

Leave Keld by the enclosed rough track at the right side of the tiny square, soon turning left at a fork to descend to a footbridge over the Swale. The path winds up past the delectable East Gill Force, where, at a junction, the Pennine Way turns left to begin its climb to Tan Hill, and our route bears right above the fall. A broad track runs impressively above the Swale Gorge, rising left at a fork to the remains of Crackpot Hall. Climbing behind the ruins the track runs along to a gate to enter the confines of Swinner Gill. A simple bridge crosses the beck below the ravine of Swinnergill Kirk, and the path turns to climb past the ruin of a smelt mill and then more stiffly up alongside East Grain.

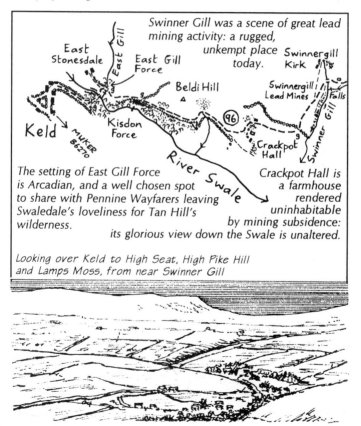

Swinner Gill was a scene of great lead mining activity: a rugged, unkempt place today.

East Stonesdale

East Gill

East Gill Force

Beldi Hill

Swinnergill Kirk

Swinnergill Lead Mines

Falls

Keld

MUKER B6270

Kisdon Force

96

River Swale

Crackpot Hall

Swinner Gill

The setting of East Gill Force is Arcadian, and a well chosen spot to share with Pennine Wayfarers leaving Swaledale's loveliness for Tan Hill's wilderness.

Crackpot Hall is a farmhouse rendered uninhabitable by mining subsidence: its glorious view down the Swale is unaltered.

Looking over Keld to High Seat, High Pike Hill and Lamps Moss, from near Swinner Gill

As the gradient eases, marshy ground and an old fold are encountered just before arriving at the shameless scar of another bulldozed shooters' track. This is crossed straight over but soon joined permanently to run - pleasantly, in parts - along the moortop to a junction on the very brow. A stonier continuation now leads along to overlook the valley of Gunnerside Gill. Beyond a stone fold, as the track swings to the right, a cairn indicates the departure of our footpath off to the left through heather, first running along the unfolding rim of North Hush's ravine before slanting down to the remains of Blakethwaite Smelt Mill.

Cross the slab bridge and take a short zigzag path directly behind the ruin to climb to a broad green way. Turn right along this lovely terraced pathway, with its good views down the well-wooded lower reaches of the gill, to drop down to a twin-cairned path junction above Bunton Crushing Mill. The path straight ahead runs past the mill and down the gill into Gunnerside, but our way is the broad one bearing gently left up the slope.

An option here is to climb rather strenuously up through the savagery of Bunton Hush to the moor above, though by far the gentler approach is to remain on the green track through a gateway, thence climb the grassy fellside near the crumbling wall. Below a sheepfold the wall is re-crossed by another green track, an increasingly broad and stony way then making the final pull onto the scarred moortop. This is now followed through a scene of untold devastation of the Old Gang Mines.

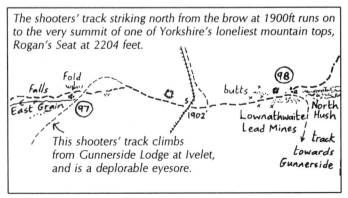

The shooters' track striking north from the brow at 1900ft runs on to the very summit of one of Yorkshire's loneliest mountain tops, Rogan's Seat at 2204 feet.

Falls

Fold

East Grain 97

98

butts

North Hush

Lownathwaite Lead Mines

1902'

track towards Gunnerside

This shooters' track climbs from Gunnerside Lodge at Ivelet, and is a deplorable eyesore.

Blakethwaite
Smelt Mill

The lead mines and ancillary workings are as much a part of
Swaledale as the waterfalls of Keld, and this side-valley of
GUNNERSIDE GILL is an excellent venue for their inspection.
Indeed, this is probably the grandest small valley in the whole of
the Dales.

Our main interest is with the Blakethwaite Smelt Mill, which was
built around 1820 to serve the mines on the moors above. Best
surviving feature is the peat store, its ruinous form looking equally
at home at Shap or Mount Grace. On the descent to and climb from
the gill, the main eye-catching features are the hushes, created by
the release of previously dammed up
water which tore away the hillside in
the search for workable veins.

Blind Gill

Blakethwaite Force

Blakethwaite Smelt Mill

Friarfold Moor

Merry Field (100)

Gunnerside Beck

Friarfold Hush

North Hush

1870'

Old Gang Lead Mines

Bunton Hush

Bunton Crushing Mill

(99)

Melbecks Moor

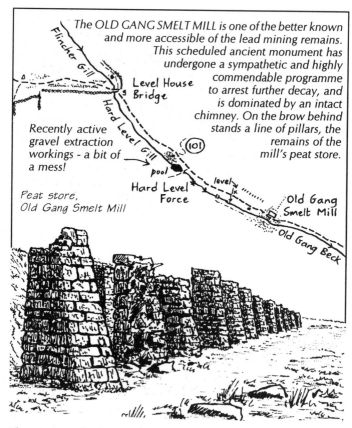

The OLD GANG SMELT MILL is one of the better known and more accessible of the lead mining remains. This scheduled ancient monument has undergone a sympathetic and highly commendable programme to arrest further decay, and is dominated by an intact chimney. On the brow behind stands a line of pillars, the remains of the mill's peat store.

Flincher Gill

Level House Bridge

Hard Level Gill

(101)

Recently active gravel extraction workings - a bit of a mess!

Peat store, Old Gang Smelt Mill

pool

Hard Level Force

level

Old Gang Smelt Mill

Old Gang Beck

The track gradually drops to meet Hard Level Gill at Level House Bridge, continuing down the side of the beck past the evocative remains of the Old Gang Smelt Mill and down to a moorland road at Surrender Bridge.

Cross straight over the road and away along a clear path, passing above the Surrender Smelt Mill and on through the heather to negotiate a crossing of the steep-walled Cringley Bottom. A stile in the wall at the other side precedes a much steadier jaunt on an increasingly clear track, with the profile of Calver Hill directly in front.

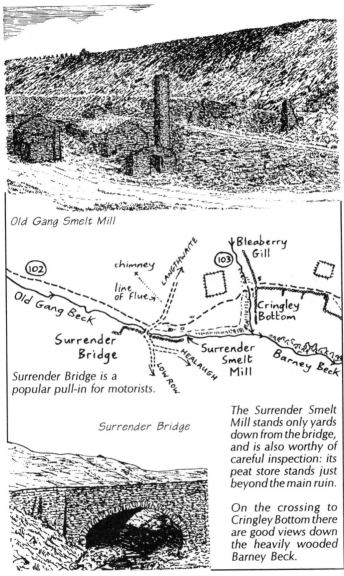

Old Gang Smelt Mill

chimney
× line of flues

102 Old Gang Beck

LANGTHWAITE

103

↓Bleaberry Gill

Cringley Bottom

Surrender Bridge

Surrender Smelt Mill

Barney Beck

HEALAUGH

LOW ROW

Surrender Bridge is a popular pull-in for motorists.

Surrender Bridge

The Surrender Smelt Mill stands only yards down from the bridge, and is also worthy of careful inspection: its peat store stands just beyond the main ruin.

On the crossing to Cringley Bottom there are good views down the heavily wooded Barney Beck.

Watersplash, Fore Gill Gate

The ford illustrated above is located just ten minutes north of Surrender Bridge, and its inclusion in the filming of a certain vet's celebrated adventures has earned it countless admirers.

Perched in the heart of grouse shooting country, Calver Hill is not the highest but is certainly the shapeliest Swaledale fell.

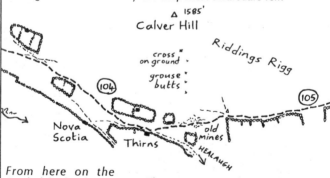

From here on the Swaledale landscape takes on a warmer, more accommodating nature.

There is a comprehensive bird's-eye view of Healaugh from the vicinity of the old mines.

The track runs along to the farm buildings of Thirns, whose access road descends to Healaugh. Attractive as it is, it has nothing to tempt us, so branch left on a rough drive climbing steeply to a cottage (Moorcock) before continuing along the front and up through old mine workings to find level ground. Calver Hill is immediately above now as the path runs across the moor, largely with a wall for company.

Above the farm of Riddings remain on the path across the moor to the next wall-corner, behind which a hidden green way known as Skelgate waits to deliver us into Reeth. Its enchanting start is soon overtaken by rather exuberant undergrowth, and whilst a riot of colour in high summer, it is not ideal in shorts. Just past a clearing either remain on Skelgate all the way down to the road, or take a stile by a gate on the right, and escape down the fields to a short snicket onto the valley road alongside the village school on the edge of Reeth.

REETH is the proud capital of Swaledale, boasting an enviable position on the lower slopes of Calver Hill. Sat high above the confluence of Arkle Beck with the Swale, it shows the greater allegiance to the former, leaving neighbouring Grinton to claim the Swale. The village centrepiece is a large, sloping green, with all buildings of importance stood respectfully back.

This one-time market town has a confident air about it, radiating largely from the hoary inns, shops and tearooms, high storeyed buildings alongside the green. Reeth caters indiscriminately for dalesfolk and visitors alike, though in the lead-mining days of the 19th century it would have been far more populous. There is an absorbing folk museum here, while agricultural shows and festivals add to the cultural attractions. On leaving Reeth, most visitors will vow to return again.

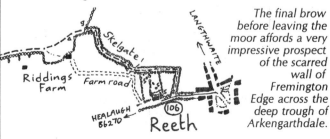

The final brow before leaving the moor affords a very impressive prospect of the scarred wall of Fremington Edge across the deep trough of Arkengarthdale.

STAGE 8

REETH to RICHMOND

11 miles

*900 feet
of ascent*

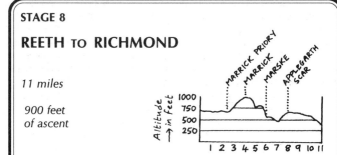

The easiest of the twelve sections is neatly incorporated in order to leave time to explore Richmond, though in truth one might set a whole day aside for that purpose. Encompassed within these few miles is an old priory, a couple of lovely villages, and a range of natural scenery from limestone scars and woodland to lush fields and leafy becks. The only wonder is why the original route let the lovely riverside section by Grinton Bridge slip the net: it's there to enjoy, and makes a far pleasanter start to the day.

If wanting to lengthen the day, consider going north from Reeth Bridge to Fremington Edge, and through Hurst and Washfold to the head of the Marske valley. A walk down this verdant vale picks up the main route in the village, while a further departure would be a riverside path that drops down from Applegarth and culminates on the opposite bank at Castle Bridge, Richmond.

Marske Hall

Leave Reeth by the Richmond road at the bottom of the green, and on crossing Reeth Bridge, look for a kissing-gate on the right. After passing alongside a farm, the path short-cuts Arkle Beck's confluence with the Swale by bearing left to a wall-corner, rounding it to a gate and aiming for Grinton Bridge. Grinton village is over the bridge, but our route only crosses the road, where a path clings to the riverbank until deflected up through trees onto the surfaced lane to Marrick Priory. Turn right on it.

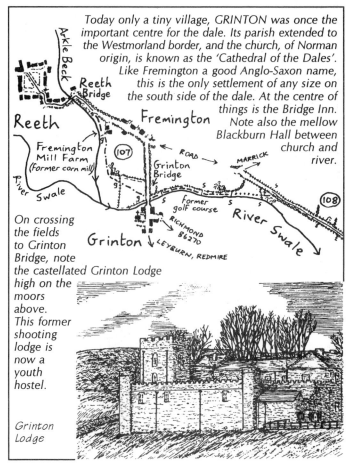

Today only a tiny village, GRINTON was once the important centre for the dale. Its parish extended to the Westmorland border, and the church, of Norman origin, is known as the 'Cathedral of the Dales'. Like Fremington a good Anglo-Saxon name, this is the only settlement of any size on the south side of the dale. At the centre of things is the Bridge Inn. Note also the mellow Blackburn Hall between church and river.

Arkle Beck

Reeth Bridge

Reeth

Fremington Mill Farm (former corn mill)

River Swale

Fremington

107

ROAD

Grinton Bridge

MARRICK

former golf course

108

River Swale

Grinton ↓ LEYBURN, REDMIRE

RICHMOND B6270

On crossing the fields to Grinton Bridge, note the castellated Grinton Lodge high on the moors above. This former shooting lodge is now a youth hostel.

Grinton Lodge

91

At the priory cross the cattle-grid and leave the farm road by a gate on the left, a short path leading to a gate into Steps Wood. A splendid, historic stone path climbs through it, the way remaining obvious to continue up to emerge as a lane into the village of Marrick. Bear right at the junction, running along to then swing left up to a junction by the phone box. Go right here (noting the sundial) to yet another junction, and take the cul-de-sac lane to the right, curving round to an early demise just past the old school. Turn left up past the adjacent house, on a short-lived green way that terminates at the first of many stiles in quick succession. The easternmost habitations of Marrick are skirted, passing a group of sheds and continuing on to a stile into a larger enclosure. At the far end things become easier, a thin path crossing meadows to descend to a farm track near Nun Cote Nook.

Use it only to pass through the gate before turning down the field to a barn, the thin path then continuing down to emerge at the front of the remarkably secluded Ellers. Cross the tiny footbridge on its far side and slant up the next two fields to join the farm road to Hollins. Turn right towards the farm, but without entering its confines turn up to the left to a stile just above the tiny wood. Slant up the next field to the top corner, continuing on a short way to a gate on the right, there crossing the brow to slant down to a stile onto a road. Turn down to the right for a prolonged descent into Marske, in view well in advance of arrival there.

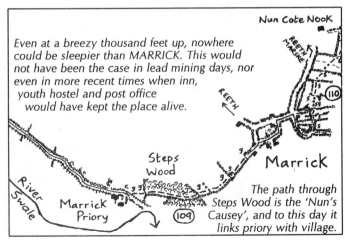

Even at a breezy thousand feet up, nowhere could be sleepier than MARRICK. This would not have been the case in lead mining days, nor even in more recent times when inn, youth hostel and post office would have kept the place alive.

Nun Cote Nook

Steps Wood

Marrick

River Swale

Marrick Priory

The path through Steps Wood is the 'Nun's Causey', and to this day it links priory with village.

On emerging onto the lane beyond Hollins are the scant remains of a sign warning of 'bulls in field on path to Marrick'. It went on to audaciously suggest an 'alternative route by road', what a damn cheek! On a brighter note, in front is the verdant upper valley of Marske Beck, a lovely sight.

Hutton's Monument recalls Matthew Hutton, a member of the once influential family of Marske Hall.

The idyllic setting of the house at Ellers remains as inaccessible as when observed by Wainwright in the early 1970s.

MARRICK PRIORY was founded in its pastoral Swaledale setting early in the 12th century to accommodate Benedictine nuns. The remains - of which the tower dominates - have been incorporated into a residential youth activity centre: visitors are welcome to have a look around the grounds.

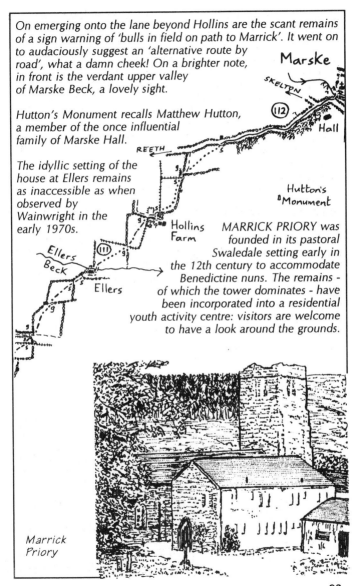

Marske

SKELTON

Hall

112

REETH

Hutton's Monument

Ellers Beck

Ellers

Hollins Farm

111

Marrick Priory

93

Applegarth Scar is a long, gleaming limestone cliff accentuated by dark foliage.

'cottage' refreshments can be obtained in Marske.

Applegarth Scar

114

West Applegarth

Clapgate Beck

RICHMOND

113

River Swale

Marske

A6108

MARSKE is a place set apart, certainly when compared to its Swaledale counterparts. Its cosy setting embowered in trees seems a far cry from a lead mining community: here is a prosperous country air of decades past. The rather austere hall is now subdued as flats, though its exterior and grounds still impress. Above the old bridge is the still older church of St. Edmund, boasting some fine Norman work.

Following the sighting at Marrick, observant collectors of sundials will reap a small harvest in Marske.

St. Edmund's, Marske

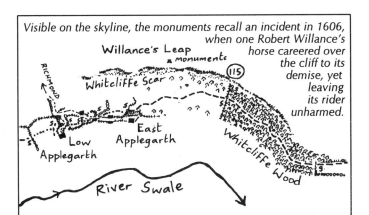

Visible on the skyline, the monuments recall an incident in 1606, when one Robert Willance's horse careered over the cliff to its demise, yet leaving its rider unharmed.

Willance's Leap
monuments
Whitcliffe Scar
115
RICHMOND
East Applegarth
Low Applegarth
Whitcliffe Wood
River Swale

The APPLEGARTH area is quite a haven from the outside world. Its string of farms is sat on a green ledge beneath the scars and high above the Swale. The only road in is the narrow access road snaking down from the old Reeth-Richmond coach road. It is here, between West and Low Applegarth, that we vacate the Yorkshire Dales National Park. East Applegarth has a camping barn. The profusion of 'no public right of way' notices in the vicinity is quite unique.

Cross Marske Bridge and rise up past the church to a junction, going right as far as the second bend left, as the road drops away. Here a stile points the way through a string of hedges before the thin path drops down to a bridge over Clapgate Beck. A clear path slants up the opposite slope to a beckoning cairn alongside a farm road. Follow it right to West Applegarth and keep straight on to a lone barn beyond it. A stile leads on past the barn and across to another stile, from where a field is crossed to emerge on the drive to Low Applegarth Farm.

Cross straight over to the next stile, and on further near the front of High Applegarth (a barn conversion) and on to the road serving East Applegarth. This is left, however, even before the farm's barns are reached, as a stile on the left points the way across a pasture well above the farm. At a stile above the farm, a clearer path runs on to meet a green cart track rising from the farm, and this is followed undulatingly through rougher, colourful country to enter Whitcliffe Wood and re-emerge on the other side.

The track runs on past High Leases, becoming surfaced for a long descent into Richmond. Above the public place of West Field one can squeeze through one of several stiles to follow a path along its top for a pleasant spell, returning to Westfields to meet the road at the edge of town. Enter the market place by crossing the road to Cravengate, then along Finkle Street and Newbiggin.

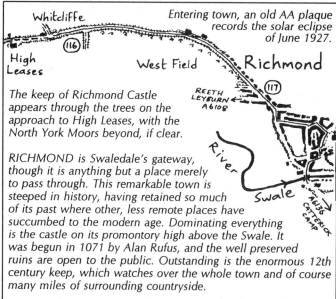

Whitcliffe

High Leases

West Field

Richmond

Entering town, an old AA plaque records the solar eclipse of June 1927.

REETH LEYBURN A6108

River

Swale

CATTERICK CAMP

The keep of Richmond Castle appears through the trees on the approach to High Leases, with the North York Moors beyond, if clear.

RICHMOND is Swaledale's gateway, though it is anything but a place merely to pass through. This remarkable town is steeped in history, having retained so much of its past where other, less remote places have succumbed to the modern age. Dominating everything is the castle on its promontory high above the Swale. It was begun in 1071 by Alan Rufus, and the well preserved ruins are open to the public. Outstanding is the enormous 12th century keep, which watches over the whole town and of course many miles of surrounding countryside.

At the very foot of the keep is the vast Market Place. At the centre of its sloping cobbles is the church of the Holy Trinity with its 14th century tower. The building uniquely incorporates a row of shops and the Green Howards Museum. Lined by shops and inns, the Market Place acts as bus station, and on Saturdays reverts to its original function. A market cross is still very much in evidence.

Outside of the square, from which numerous wynds (narrow ways) radiate, is the parish church of St.Mary, with another 14th century tower and 16th century stalls. Also in the vicinity is the upstanding Grey Friars Tower, across the road from the Georgian Theatre. This fascinating place dates from 1788, and has been restored to perform its intended role again. The strong military presence in the town is due to the proximity of the vast Catterick Camp.

Richmond Castle from Castle Bridge

STAGE 9

RICHMOND TO INGLEBY CROSS

23 miles   *500 feet of ascent*

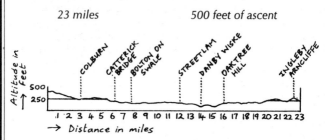

The longest section on offer, this near-marathon crossing of the Vale of Mowbray gets you from the Dales to the Moors in one fell swoop, a worthy objective if you've a liking for elevated ground. Certainly there are features of interest, though if this is all for one day then really you don't want too many distractions! The Swale itself provides early company, while there are moments to break the monotony at Bolton on Swale and Danby Wiske.

Although the amount of road walking is a little less than it once was, there are nevertheless a good few miles of tarmac bashing. The advantages, however, are several: faster progress is a major one, for if gobbling all this up in one day, the likelihood is that paths around three sides of a cornfield would only be abandoned in order to maintain a reasonable bee-line; the roads are in any case virtually traffic-free; one should be in reasonable shape if the previous day was only the suggested stroll from Reeth.

Options to shorten the walking are naturally few, though one could get off to a flyer by eschewing the intricate early miles in favour of a route by way of Easby Abbey and Brompton on Swale, mapped on the following pages; certainly Easby Abbey and its lovely environs deserve a visit. A short-cut from Danby Lane to Oaktree Hill makes a small but welcome break from the original route. If bound for Osmotherley, one could significantly shorten things by leaving Long Lane in favour of a route by Low Moor and Harlsey Castle.

From the Market Place's south-west corner descend charming streets to cross Castle Bridge. Follow the Swale downstream past sports fields (magnificent views of the castle) into woodland, the path soon rising into a field. Go left and locate a stile on the right, as the more obvious way runs on towards Station Bridge: our path rises between barns to pass along the front of a row of houses. At the main road go right, out of town. When it swings right, after a private drive, take a waterworks road doubling back to the left. At the works the path bears right to run outside its boundary.

On entering woodland the way soon forks, though merging again at a footbridge. The path climbs to the wood-top and along to a stile, escaping to reach ruinous Hagg Farm. Go left along a stony track, fading at a gate where a thin trod rises across the field. Continue over the brow in the next field to a stile at the far corner, then bear left down a field-side.

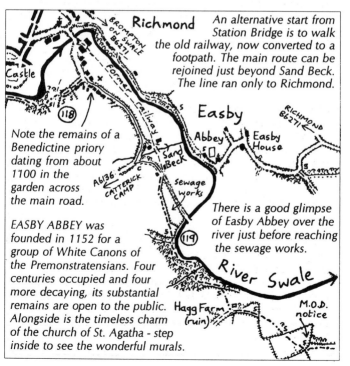

An alternative start from Station Bridge is to walk the old railway, now converted to a footpath. The main route can be rejoined just beyond Sand Beck. The line ran only to Richmond.

Note the remains of a Benedictine priory dating from about 1100 in the garden across the main road.

EASBY ABBEY was founded in 1152 for a group of White Canons of the Premonstratensians. Four centuries occupied and four more decaying, its substantial remains are open to the public. Alongside is the timeless charm of the church of St. Agatha - step inside to see the wonderful murals.

There is a good glimpse of Easby Abbey over the river just before reaching the sewage works.

The Swale at Catterick Bridge

ST. GILES HOSPITAL was one of a number run under monastic orders, and date from the late 12th century. Excavations in 1990 revealed skeletons galore - removed to York for further research before river erosion washes it away! By the riverbank are the scant remains of the chapel, while on the banktop are numerous grassy earthworks of ancillary buildings. The site was abandoned over 500 years ago, though was later occupied by a farm, fore-runner of the present one up above.

Our acquaintance with COLBURN is limited to the old village, to which a larger, modern appendage has been added nearer Catterick Camp. Village pub is the Hildyard Arms. Pass slowly through the farmyard leaving the village, its range of farm buildings possess unusual architectural merit.

At the bottom corner of the field bear slightly right to locate a part-hidden stile into the trees. A clear path now accompanies a small beck to emerge onto a drive, there turning right to enter sleepy Colburn. Cross the road bridge almost opposite and head along the street past the pub. At the end go straight ahead, turning sharp right into a farmyard, then left along a cart-track.

Part-way along, turn left on a fainter way alongside a hedge, then continue high above a wooded bank of the river. As the way opens out bear right with a fence, passing near an information panel inviting a look at the medieval hospital site. Rise gradually to by-pass St. Giles Farm and emerge onto its drive. Almost at once however, go left after a cattle-grid with a fence above a wooded bank, and from a stile at the end head along the bank top to join a cart-track leading to Thornbrough. Alongside the farm buildings, slip down to the left to discover the A1 just below!

Pass under the pulsating highway and a defunct railway bridge to rise slightly right to a stile onto the old A1 opposite the race-course. Go left past the hotel and cross the bridge with care. Immediately over, take a stile on the right to follow the riverbank. A generally clear path accompanies either the Swale itself or, for a time, a crumbling wall alongside a scrubby area.

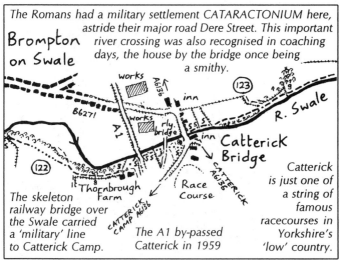

The Romans had a military settlement CATARACTONIUM here, astride their major road Dere Street. This important river crossing was also recognised in coaching days, the house by the bridge once being a smithy.

Brompton on Swale

works

A636

inn

(123)

B6271

works

A1

rly bridge

inn

Catterick Bridge

R. Swale

(122)

Thornbrough Farm

CATTERICK CAMP A6136

Race Course

CATTERICK A6136

The skeleton railway bridge over the Swale carried a 'military' line to Catterick Camp.

The A1 by-passed Catterick in 1959

Catterick is just one of a string of famous racecourses in Yorkshire's 'low' country.

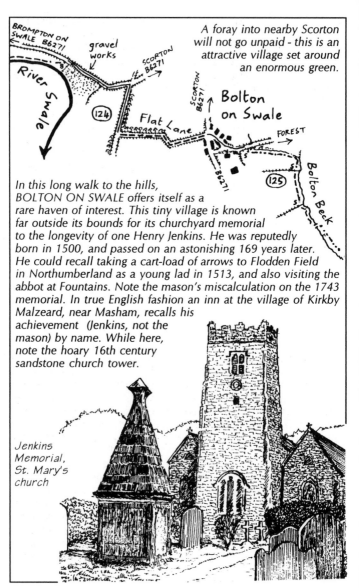

BROMPTON ON SWALE B6271

gravel works

SCORTON B6271

River Swale

124

Flat Lane

SCORTON B6271

Bolton on Swale

FOREST

B6271

125

Bolton Beck

A foray into nearby Scorton will not go unpaid - this is an attractive village set around an enormous green.

In this long walk to the hills, BOLTON ON SWALE offers itself as a rare haven of interest. This tiny village is known far outside its bounds for its churchyard memorial to the longevity of one Henry Jenkins. He was reputedly born in 1500, and passed on an astonishing 169 years later. He could recall taking a cart-load of arrows to Flodden Field in Northumberland as a young lad in 1513, and also visiting the abbot at Fountains. Note the mason's miscalculation on the 1743 memorial. In true English fashion an inn at the village of Kirkby Malzeard, near Masham, recalls his achievement (Jenkins, not the mason) by name. While here, note the hoary 16th century sandstone church tower.

Jenkins Memorial, St. Mary's church

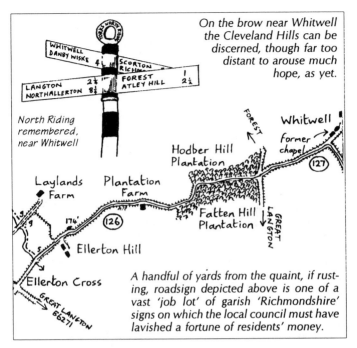

On the brow near Whitwell the Cleveland Hills can be discerned, though far too distant to arouse much hope, as yet.

North Riding remembered, near Whitwell

A handful of yards from the quaint, if rusting, roadsign depicted above is one of a vast 'job lot' of garish 'Richmondshire' signs on which the local council must have lavished a fortune of residents' money.

Approaching a gravel works the pleasant riverbank path slants across this long field up onto the B6271. Go right a short way (footway) until at the first chance turn down a lane on the right (the houses ahead belong to Catterick village, across the river). Again at the first chance, turn left along a rough lane to emerge back onto the B6271 at Bolton on Swale. Cross straight over and head for the church, passing the preserved village pump en route.

At the church bear left along the road, and at an early stile bear left across the field, accompanying a charming stream meandering through the fields. At the far corner the beck-side is traced up to a crumbling stone bridge - a pleasing setting for a snack - crossing it and continuing upstream across a farm drive and along to a stile onto a road at Ellerton Hill. This same road is now followed (left) all the way to Streetlam, enjoying a spell amidst plantations and making rapid, traffic-free progress towards a lunchtime halt.

A name on the OS map just north of Streetlam conjures up a vision of everything we're missing, for despite its wilder connotations, *FELL GILL MOOR* promises all and delivers nowt.

The walk to Whitwell Moor is actually a
   discernible pull,
     relatively speaking!

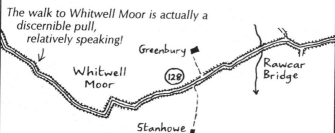

DANBY WISKE has earned for itself a modest reputation as the only staging post on the long haul to Ingleby Cross. It is the most peaceful of communities, though the site of booted legions striding through is no longer a bizarre apparition to its residents. Indeed, Danby Wiske is a veritable haven, with the opportunity for a pint on the green, or, on the outskirts, tea on the lawn. It may well be the lowest point between the two seashores, but it certainly does its best. Even the pub sign sports the mileages to each coast!

Just down the lane is its attractive church, which incorporates work from many periods, all the way back to Norman origins.

The White Swan, Danby Wiske

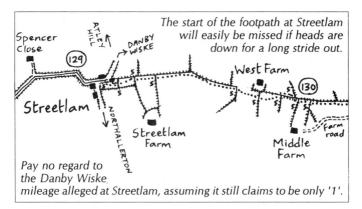

The start of the footpath at Streetlam will easily be missed if heads are down for a long stride out.

Spencer Close

129

BATLEY HILL

DANBY WISKE

West Farm

130

Streetlam

NORTHALLERTON

Streetlam Farm

Middle Farm

farm road

Pay no regard to the Danby Wiske mileage alleged at Streetlam, assuming it still claims to be only '1'.

At the road junction in Streetlam an obvious improvement to the original route awaits in the form of a respite from the tarmac. Just on the corner is a stile, for a direct line treks across numerous fields, beyond the initial paddocks the way simply keeping to the left-hand field boundary. These pleasant sheep pastures are marginally shorter if no quicker, but certainly gentler on the feet. At the other end a farm road is joined to lead back onto the original road, now just minutes out of Danby Wiske, descending Park Hill into the village. With these miles of tarmac the warning of 'no footway for 400 yards' should not be taken too seriously.

Leave Danby by keeping straight on the road, bridging the snaking Wiske and, a little beyond, the railway line.

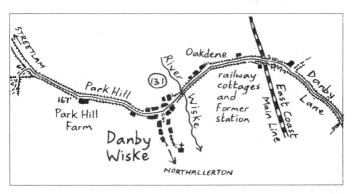

STREETLAM

Oakdene

River Wiske

railway cottages and former station

Danby Lane

Park Hill

131

East Coast Main Line

167'

Park Hill Farm

Danby Wiske

NORTHALLERTON

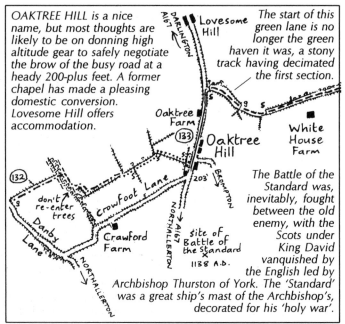

OAKTREE HILL is a nice name, but most thoughts are likely to be on donning high altitude gear to safely negotiate the brow of the busy road at a heady 200-plus feet. A former chapel has made a pleasing domestic conversion. Lovesome Hill offers accommodation.

The start of this green lane is no longer the green haven it was, a stony track having decimated the first section.

The Battle of the Standard was, inevitably, fought between the old enemy, with the Scots under King David vanquished by the English led by Archbishop Thurston of York. The 'Standard' was a great ship's mast of the Archbishop's, decorated for his 'holy war'.

The old route remains on Danby Lane to a junction for Oaktree Hill. A more direct way leaves a gate on the left opposite a drive to Lazenby Hall Farm. At the far end pass through a thicket, bear right around the field-side to the bottom corner: continue away to successive stiles before rising right with a hedge to join the A167. Cross to the Oak Tree Garage, and go left on the verge past Oak Tree Farm to escape by a stile on the right. A rough track heads away, soon becoming a tightly enclosed footway which gradually broadens to join Deighton Lane.

Go left only as far as a drive branching right to Moor House Farm. Keep straight on between the buildings then slant left to a stile. Follow the winding field-side around to locate a stile opposite, then on to bridge a tiny stream. Head away past Brompton Moor Farm to the far corner, then run along to another streamlet before the path strikes directly ahead for the hotch-potch of buildings of Northfield Farm. Keep left of them all to a stile, then straight ahead to the next stile to join the farm road. Go left past Northfield House and out onto another road.

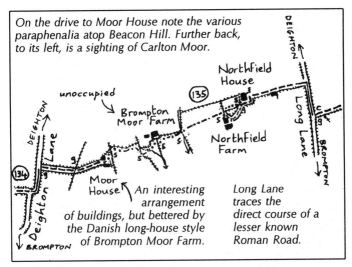

On the drive to Moor House note the various paraphenalia atop Beacon Hill. Further back, to its left, is a sighting of Carlton Moor.

unoccupied

Northfield House

(135)

Brompton Moor Farm

DEIGHTON

Long Lane

DEIGHTON

Northfield Farm

BROMPTON

(134)

Moor House

An interesting arrangement of buildings, but bettered by the Danish long-house style of Brompton Moor Farm.

Deighton Lane

BROMPTON

Long Lane traces the direct course of a lesser known Roman Road.

Turn briefly right then branch left along the drive to Wray House. Once again neatly avoiding a farmyard, go right down a very short-lived way to debouch into a field with a railway ahead. Bear well to the left to a crossing, then head straight down the field to a footbridge and then a plank in a field corner. Its boundary is now followed left around two sides to join Low Moor Lane. Go left to approach the farmstead of Harlsey Grove, and when it turns in to it, bear right on the rougher continuation of Low Moor Lane.

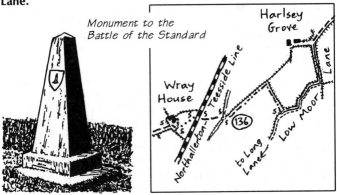

Monument to the Battle of the Standard

Harlsey Grove

Wray House

Northallerton–Teesside Line

Low Moor Lane

(136)

to Long Lane

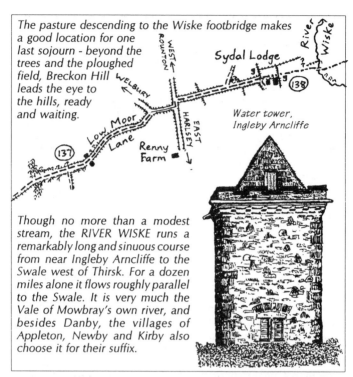

The pasture descending to the Wiske footbridge makes a good location for one last sojourn - beyond the trees and the ploughed field, Breckon Hill leads the eye to the hills, ready and waiting.

WEST ROUNTON

WELBURY

Sydal Lodge

River Wiske

Low Moor Lane

EAST HARLSEY

137

Renny Farm

Water tower, Ingleby Arncliffe

138

Though no more than a modest stream, the RIVER WISKE runs a remarkably long and sinuous course from near Ingleby Arncliffe to the Swale west of Thirsk. For a dozen miles alone it flows roughly parallel to the Swale. It is very much the Vale of Mowbray's own river, and besides Danby, the villages of Appleton, Newby and Kirby also choose it for their suffix.

A long trek along Low Moor Lane leads out to a surfaced road. Go right to the junction then left, only to turn right almost at once along the drive to Sydal Lodge. Go straight ahead, left of all buildings, and keep on again to a gate. The path heads away with the ruin of Breckon Hill a sure guide straight ahead, and the Cleveland Hills now almost touchable behind.

The path descends to a footbridge (the lazy Wiske again) and then climbs to Breckon Hill, passing to the right of the crumbling remains to follow the drive out. The buzz of traffic on the A19 is heard as the drive zigzags past two farms to emerge onto the highway alongside a filling station and a cafe. A dual carriageway is of benefit on this final hairy crossing to a contrastingly narrow lane rising to Ingleby Arncliffe. At the staggered junction keep on to descend the road into Ingleby Cross.

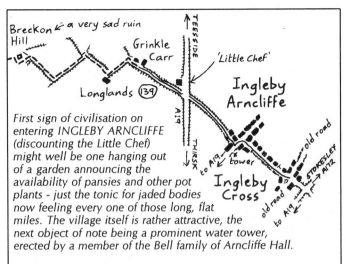

Breckon Hill ← a very sad ruin

Grinkle Carr

'Little Chef'

Ingleby Arncliffe

TEESSIDE

THIRSK

A19

to A19 → tower

Longlands (139)

old road

STOKESLEY A172

Ingleby Cross

old road

to A19 →

First sign of civilisation on entering INGLEBY ARNCLIFFE (discounting the Little Chef) might well be one hanging out of a garden announcing the availability of pansies and other pot plants - just the tonic for jaded bodies now feeling every one of those long, flat miles. The village itself is rather attractive, the next object of note being a prominent water tower, erected by a member of the Bell family of Arncliffe Hall.

Long since gratefully by-passed, INGLEBY CROSS is the 'business' partner. Its 'cross' (a war memorial), its comfortable Blue Bell Inn, its tiny post office, its village hall and all its cottages enjoy a peace disturbed only by the occasional Northallerton-Stokesley bus and the exhausted walkers abandoned on its welcoming green.

MOUNT GRACE PRIORY (see overleaf) was founded in 1398, and now forms the most extensive Carthusian remains in the country. In wooded seclusion beneath Beacon Hill, it is a National Trust property administered by English Heritage. Of special interest are the rows of cells, where the monks would have little difficulty in maintaining their vows of silence.

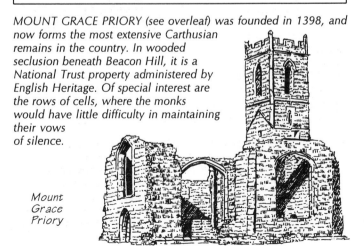

Mount Grace Priory

STAGE 10

INGLEBY CROSS
TO
CLAY BANK TOP

12 miles

*2700 feet
of ascent*

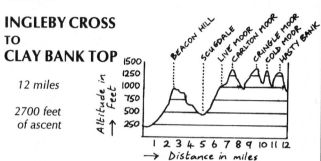

Growing ever nearer yesterday, the Cleveland Hills are now underfoot, and this is a day to savour, incorporating the most famous dozen miles on the North York Moors. The crossing of the escarpment has superb views not only out to the Cleveland Plain and into the heart of the moors, but also of the ever changing aspects of the day's hills. Though the miles are few and the route clear, this is quite a roller-coaster. Rather than trying to press on beyond Clay Bank Top, it is recommended to take your time, include a visit to the majestic Mount Grace Priory, and finish with a downhill stroll into Great Broughton. With luck your host will even deposit you back on Clay Bank Top after breakfast.

A lower level alternative uses lanes and field-paths north of the escarpment, by way of Swainby, Faceby and Carlton. The route could be picked up on Carlton Bank to follow the jet miners' track. If crossing Clay Bank Top is not important, then a further option cuts through Scugdale and over to Chop Gate, there taking a track onto Urra Moor to pick up the route on Round Hill.

Old guidepost under Cringle Moor

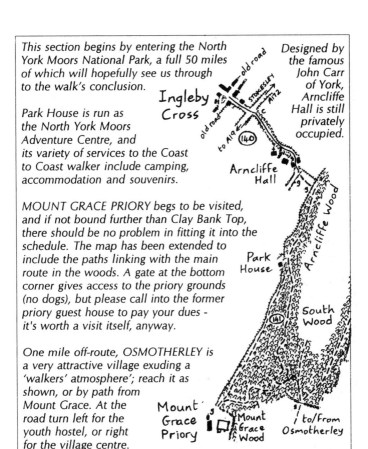

This section begins by entering the North York Moors National Park, a full 50 miles of which will hopefully see us through to the walk's conclusion.

Ingleby Cross

Designed by the famous John Carr of York, Arncliffe Hall is still privately occupied.

Park House is run as the North York Moors Adventure Centre, and its variety of services to the Coast to Coast walker include camping, accommodation and souvenirs.

MOUNT GRACE PRIORY begs to be visited, and if not bound further than Clay Bank Top, there should be no problem in fitting it into the schedule. The map has been extended to include the paths linking with the main route in the woods. A gate at the bottom corner gives access to the priory grounds (no dogs), but please call into the former priory guest house to pay your dues - it's worth a visit itself, anyway.

One mile off-route, OSMOTHERLEY is a very attractive village exuding a 'walkers' atmosphere'; reach it as shown, or by path from Mount Grace. At the road turn left for the youth hostel, or right for the village centre.

Arncliffe Hall

Park House

Arncliffe Wood

South Wood

Mount Grace Priory

Mount Grace Wood

to/from Osmotherley

From the green head past the *Blue Bell* and out onto the A172. Cross over and head along the leafy lane past Arncliffe Church and Hall, then up the hill take a gate on the left to follow a track up to Arncliffe Wood. Turn right along the forest road, passing above Park House and then deeper into the woods. The way remains clear, swinging up to a T-junction and there rising to the right to the edge of the wood. The gate in front signals our merging with the Cleveland Way coming out from Osmotherley, but without leaving the wood turn sharply up to the left on a clear path rising through South Wood.

At the top of the wood the path runs along a wallside, past an incongruous booster station and the Ordnance column atop Beacon Hill. A little beyond, the way emerges onto a corner of Scarth Wood Moor, a glorious moment. In the distance is the conical peak of Roseberry Topping, but nearer to hand is a striking array of moors that form the greater part of the day - an exciting prospect indeed.

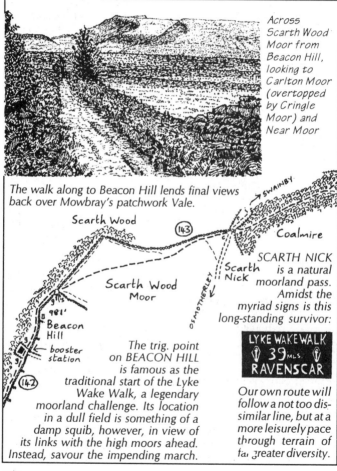

Across Scarth Wood Moor from Beacon Hill, looking to Carlton Moor (overtopped by Cringle Moor) and Near Moor

The walk along to Beacon Hill lends final views back over Mowbray's patchwork Vale.

Scarth Wood

(143)

Coalmire

→ SWAINBY

Scarth Wood Moor

Scarth Nick

OSMOTHERLEY

981'
Beacon Hill

← booster station

(142)

SCARTH NICK is a natural moorland pass. Amidst the myriad signs is this long-standing survivor:

The trig. point on BEACON HILL is famous as the traditional start of the Lyke Wake Walk, a legendary moorland challenge. Its location in a dull field is something of a damp squib, however, in view of its links with the high moors ahead. Instead, savour the impending march.

LYKE WAKE WALK
⚰ 39 MLS. ⚰
RAVENSCAR

Our own route will follow a not too dissimilar line, but at a more leisurely pace through terrain of far greater diversity.

Above Huthwaite Green, SCUGDALE is a lovely valley deeply inurned between high moors, and is seen to good advantage from the top of Live Moor. In the past it was mined for jet and ironstone, with a railway line constructed to convey the latter out of the dale. Some outstanding bluebell woods precede arrival in Scugdale. Huthwaite Green's entertainment value is limited to what might be achieved in a phone box. If in dire need of sustenance, Swainby is a mile and a half distant.

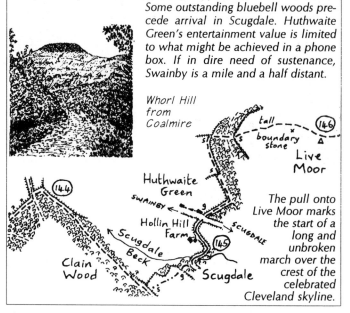

Whorl Hill from Coalmire

Live Moor

Huthwaite Green

The pull onto Live Moor marks the start of a long and unbroken march over the crest of the celebrated Cleveland skyline.

The main path crosses the moor diagonally to descend onto the road through Scarth Nick, and across the cattle-grid take a gate into the plantation. A path heads off to quickly join a forest road through Coalmire, which is left at a fork by dropping steeply to the left. At a staggered crossroads go left a couple of yards and then sharp right, a clear path running along the foot of Clain Wood. In lovely surroundings a stile on the left signals time to leave the broad path by descending a field to a rough track fording Scugdale Beck. On the other side a narrow lane leads up to the left to a junction at Huthwaite Green.

Cross straight over and up an enclosed path past the phone box, swinging left along the base of a plantation until a stile admits to a steep climb through the trees. The open moor is quickly gained, and a pleasant climb continues over the brow of Live Moor.

113

Summit of Carlton Moor, looking ahead to Cringle Moor

From Live Moor to CARLTON MOOR the track is visible all the way ahead, the steep western flank contrasting well with the heather carpet of the moortop. In the fashion of its ensuing colleagues, Carlton Moor rises gently from the south to an abrupt top overlooking the Cleveland Plain. Select a heathery couch and with the aid of a map, try to identify the villages outspread. The nearest, appropriately, is Carlton.

On Cringle End

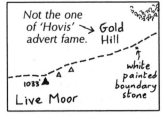

Arrival on CRINGLE END is a champagne moment: aside from the ever-present views over the Cleveland Plain to the peak of Roseberry Topping, the highlight is the sudden appearance of Cringle's north face plunging dramatically to the lower contours, with both Cold Moor and Hasty Bank making their appearances in some style. The 'furniture' confirms this as a compulsory halt, one of those indefinable 'good places to be'.

114

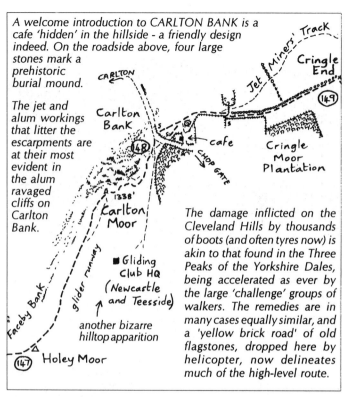

A welcome introduction to CARLTON BANK is a cafe 'hidden' in the hillside - a friendly design indeed. On the roadside above, four large stones mark a prehistoric burial mound.

The jet and alum workings that litter the escarpments are at their most evident in the alum ravaged cliffs on Carlton Bank.

CARLTON

Carlton Bank

Jet Miners' Track

Cringle End

149

cafe

Cringle Moor Plantation

CHOP GATE

148

1338'

Carlton Moor

■ Gliding Club HQ (Newcastle and Teesside)

another bizarre hilltop apparition

glider runway

Faceby Bank

147 △ Holey Moor

The damage inflicted on the Cleveland Hills by thousands of boots (and often tyres now) is akin to that found in the Three Peaks of the Yorkshire Dales, being accelerated as ever by the large 'challenge' groups of walkers. The remedies are in many cases equally similar, and a 'yellow brick road' of old flagstones, dropped here by helicopter, now delineates much of the high-level route.

The path runs along the crest of Live Moor and onto waiting Carlton Moor: the final section is sandwiched between the escarpment to the left and a glider runway to the right. The summit is marked by an Ordnance column and a tall boundary stone, a good place to halt. Caution is needed on the descent, where the path has been re-routed away from the precipitous drops into the alum quarries that scar the northern face of the hill. Cringle Moor waits patiently opposite, the crossing being interrupted by the Carlton-Chop Gate road on Carlton Bank.

Across the road a path runs happily along before a short pull onto Cringle End, where another boundary stone stands alongside a memorial view indicator and seat.

*Cringle Moor from Cringle End,
looking to Hasty Bank, Cold Moor and distant Urra Moor*

The lower-level track can be picked up in this gap for a more sheltered trek along the top of the plantations.

Jet Miners' Track

(150) shelter

Garfit Gap

▲ 1319' Cold Moor

old mine level

stone guidepost

1417' ▲ Drake Howe (tumulus)
Cringle Moor

CRINGLE MOOR is second only to Urra Moor's Round Hill in the hierarchy of the Moors, yet its summit is the only one along this escarpment that is omitted, being set well back amidst trackless heather.

COLD MOOR points a slender finger south to Bilsdale, and from its tiny cairn a very inviting path sets off through the heather. Along with ironstone and alum, these hills were also plundered for jet (of 'jet black' fame), at one time a popular ornamental stone. Evidence of the old mines is most apparent when looking back to Cringle Moor from Cold Moor - just select the right contour.

HASTY BANK may not be the highest point on the Cleveland ridge, but it is arguably the finest. The northern scarp, in addition to its greater length, falls away in a series of superior cliffs: stride carefully here!

From Cringle End the path rises a little further, in dramatic fashion along the escarpment just below Cringle Moor's summit. A steep descent follows to the depression in front of Cold Moor, where a wall is followed up then crossed for the short climb to its cairn. The descent is equally rapid, spurred on by the prospect of the Wainstones on Hasty Bank, final summit before Clay Bank Top.

A short climb is followed by an easy clamber up between the pinnacles, and then a long crossing of Hasty Bank's broad top. When its northern scarp subsides, the inevitable steep descent runs down to the top of the plantations that cloak the northern slopes, and a wallside path culminates in steps dropping the final yards onto the road summit at Clay Bank Top.

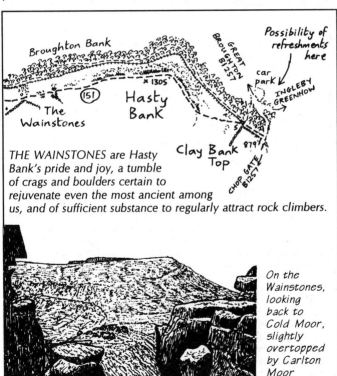

Broughton Bank

GREAT BROUGHTON B1257

Possibility of refreshments here

car park

INGLEBY GREENHOW

× 1305

(151)

Hasty Bank

The Wainstones

Clay Bank Top

879'

CHOP GATE B1257

THE WAINSTONES are Hasty Bank's pride and joy, a tumble of crags and boulders certain to rejuvenate even the most ancient among us, and of sufficient substance to regularly attract rock climbers.

On the Wainstones, looking back to Cold Moor, slightly overtopped by Carlton Moor

STAGE 11

CLAY BANK TOP TO GLAISDALE

18½ miles *1000 feet of ascent*

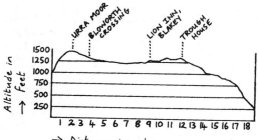

Considering that going on for a dozen miles are spent above the 1250ft contour, the walking on this section is supremely effortless. Only the very first half-mile pull onto Urra Moor offers any resistance, after which broad strides, broad tracks and even broader sweeps of moorland are the order of the day. Beyond the summit of the moors on Round Hill, the Rosedale ironstone railway trackbed is picked up at Bloworth Crossing, and winds a well engineered course around the head of Farndale before throwing us off at Blakey. Here the *Lion Inn*, only habitation of the day, awaits our thirsts, and beyond the heart of the moors at Rosedale Head, with its crosses and various stones, the way resumes around the magnificent head of Great Fryup Dale, a tributary of the Esk to which the long declining miles of Glaisdale Rigg will lead.

No obvious alternatives present themselves, and none should be necessary. More circuitous routes could be devised by breaking off earlier for Eskdale, either from Bloworth to Baysdale and thence Castleton, or down into Great Fryup Dale for Lealholm. One could also drop south into Farndale, though this would only be practicable if seeking a bed there.

Leave the road summit by Hagg's Gate opposite, from where a restored path rises, steeply in the earlier stages, onto the heather of Urra Moor. Lined by innumerable boundary stones it becomes a Landrover track well before reaching the Ordnance column on Round Hill, just off to the left from the Hand Stone.

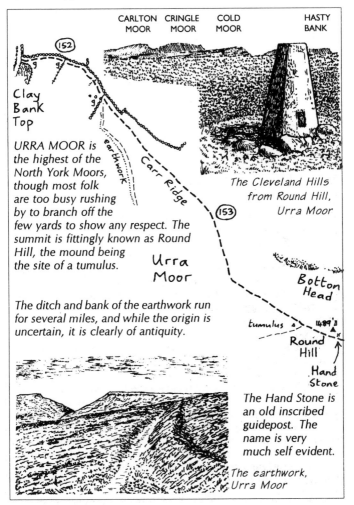

CARLTON MOOR   CRINGLE MOOR   COLD MOOR   HASTY BANK

(152)

Clay Bank Top

earthwork

Carr Ridge

(153)

URRA MOOR is the highest of the North York Moors, though most folk are too busy rushing by to branch off the few yards to show any respect. The summit is fittingly known as Round Hill, the mound being the site of a tumulus.

Urra Moor

The ditch and bank of the earthwork run for several miles, and while the origin is uncertain, it is clearly of antiquity.

The Cleveland Hills from Round Hill, Urra Moor

Botton Head

tumulus ▲   1489'▲

Round Hill

Hand Stone

The Hand Stone is an old inscribed guidepost. The name is very much self evident.

The earthwork, Urra Moor

119

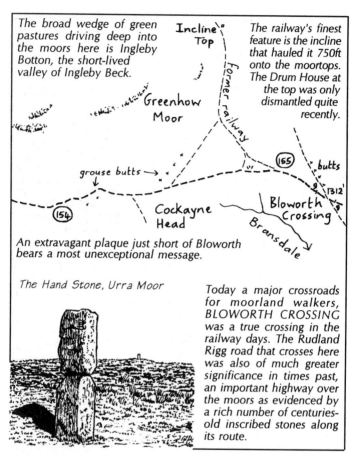

The broad wedge of green pastures driving deep into the moors here is Ingleby Botton, the short-lived valley of Ingleby Beck.

Incline Top

former railway

The railway's finest feature is the incline that hauled it 750ft onto the moortops. The Drum House at the top was only dismantled quite recently.

Greenhow Moor

grouse butts →

155

butts

1312

154

Cockayne Head

Bloworth Crossing

Bransdale

An extravagant plaque just short of Bloworth bears a most unexceptional message.

The Hand Stone, Urra Moor

Today a major crossroads for moorland walkers, BLOWORTH CROSSING was a true crossing in the railway days. The Rudland Rigg road that crosses here was also of much greater significance in times past, an important highway over the moors as evidenced by a rich number of centuries-old inscribed stones along its route.

Beyond Round Hill the track makes a steady descent towards the former Rosedale Ironstone Railway, whose course is discerned well before it is joined. Just short of it our track swings left, but keep straight on the path to merge into the trackbed. Only a little further is Bloworth Crossing. Here we take our leave of the Cleveland Way, which turns sharply to follow the old road north, while we continue to take advantage of the trackbed for no less than five further miles, contouring around the head of Farndale and its many infant streams.

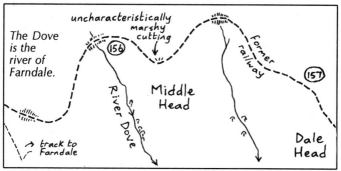

The Dove is the river of Farndale.

uncharacteristically marshy cutting

156

former railway

157

River Dove

Middle Head

Dale Head

track to Farndale

From Bloworth Crossing to beneath the Lion Inn on Blakey Ridge, we follow the trackbed of the ROSEDALE IRONSTONE RAILWAY. It was built in 1861 to convey ironstone from Rosedale, in the heart of the moors, out over the watershed and down to the furnaces of Teesside. This remarkable feat of engineering saw trains cross the moors at 1300ft. With the demise of the industry the line closed in 1929, and today it is difficult to visualise either the trains or the thousands labouring hard in now tranquil Rosedale.

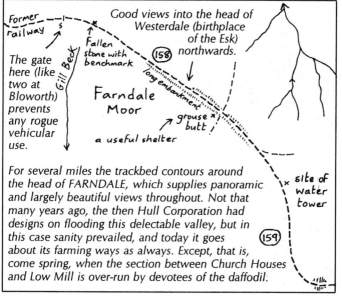

Former railway

Good views into the head of Westerdale (birthplace of the Esk) northwards.

Fallen stone with benchmark

Gill Beck

158

long embankment

The gate here (like two at Bloworth) prevents any rogue vehicular use.

Farndale Moor

grouse butt

a useful shelter

site of water tower

159

For several miles the trackbed contours around the head of FARNDALE, which supplies panoramic and largely beautiful views throughout. Not that many years ago, the then Hull Corporation had designs on flooding this delectable valley, but in this case sanity prevailed, and today it goes about its farming ways as always. Except, that is, come spring, when the section between Church Houses and Low Mill is over-run by devotees of the daffodil.

At a final cutting the *Lion Inn* at Blakey appears inspiringly on the skyline ahead. The head of one last side-valley is rounded before a clear path strikes off left to climb through the heather up to a wallside and the standing stone on Blakey Howe, immediately above the hostelry. Beyond the moor road is the head of Rosedale, and while the rail track heads that way, it does so without us. Few will resist a break at the *Lion*, first opportunity for en-route alcohol since Osmotherley.

Emerging blinking into the daylight, turn left along the capacious verge for a mile as far as a large, ungainly stone on the left known as Margery Bradley. Here a path strikes off to the right through heather, cutting the corner of the road junction at Rosedale Head to meet the Rosedale Abbey road at the prominent White Cross.

The Lion Inn, Blakey

THE LION INN dates back over 400 years, and while it was once frequented by ironstone and coal miners, today it is a prominent landmark waylaying most of the walkers and tourists who pass by. The highway it services carries a surprising volume of traffic considering it is a humble moorland road: the answer lies in it being an ideal and rare link between villages in the north and south of the Park, without severe gradients and corners.

South of the Lion is Blakey Junction, where the former railway divided for either Rosedale West Mines, or to encircle Rosedale Head for several miles more to Rosedale East Mines.

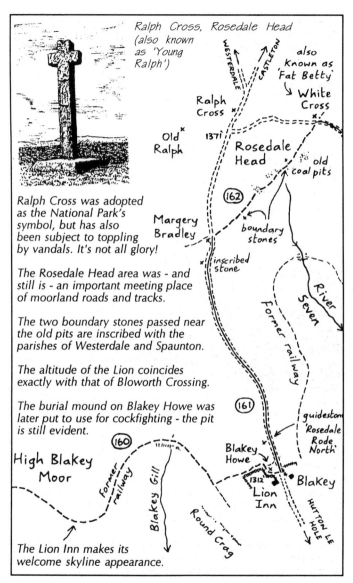

Ralph Cross, Rosedale Head (also known as 'Young Ralph')

also known as 'Fat Betty' → White Cross

Ralph Cross ×

Old Ralph ×

137¹

Rosedale Head ×

old coal pits

(162)

Margery Bradley ×

boundary stones

× inscribed stone

Ralph Cross was adopted as the National Park's symbol, but has also been subject to toppling by vandals. It's not all glory!

The Rosedale Head area was - and still is - an important meeting place of moorland roads and tracks.

The two boundary stones passed near the old pits are inscribed with the parishes of Westerdale and Spaunton.

The altitude of the Lion coincides exactly with that of Bloworth Crossing.

The burial mound on Blakey Howe was later put to use for cockfighting - the pit is still evident.

River Seven

former railway

(161)

guidestone 'Rosedale Rode North'

(160)

High Blakey Moor

former railway

Blakey Gill

Round Crag

Blakey Howe ×

1312 ×

Lion Inn

Blakey

HUTTON LE HOLE

The Lion Inn makes its welcome skyline appearance.

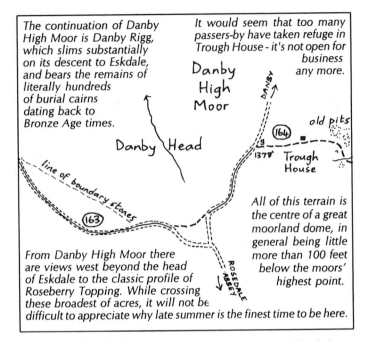

The continuation of Danby High Moor is Danby Rigg, which slims substantially on its descent to Eskdale, and bears the remains of literally hundreds of burial cairns dating back to Bronze Age times.

It would seem that too many passers-by have taken refuge in Trough House - it's not open for business any more.

Danby High Moor

DANBY

old pits

164

Danby Head

1378' Trough House

line of boundary stones

163

From Danby High Moor there are views west beyond the head of Eskdale to the classic profile of Roseberry Topping. While crossing these broadest of acres, it will not be difficult to appreciate why late summer is the finest time to be here.

All of this terrain is the centre of a great moorland dome, in general being little more than 100 feet below the moors' highest point.

ROSEDALE ABBEY

The route turns right for ten minutes, though an unofficial short-cut forks left to trace a chain of boundary stones (the moist nature of the peat means there is no saving in time). After it rejoins the road, the route proper leaves it only a minute or so later, a thin, clear path cutting a corner to emerge on a single-track road branching down to the left for Little Fryup Dale. This is followed over a gentle brow with distant Eskdale outspread, and as Trough House appears, a track branches off for it. Beyond the shooting hut the way encounters the headwaters of Great Fryup Beck, there encircling in grand style the head of Great Fryup Dale.

This is a splendid section, the heather surrounds of many miles being enhanced by the addition of bilberry and some bracken, while the colourful and rough-fashioned dalehead drops steeply away to the left. Continuing on, the broad path eventually filters onto a moorland road, with the valley of Glaisdale reaching away in front. Turn left as far as a broad track branching straight ahead as the road swings left to a white Ordnance column.

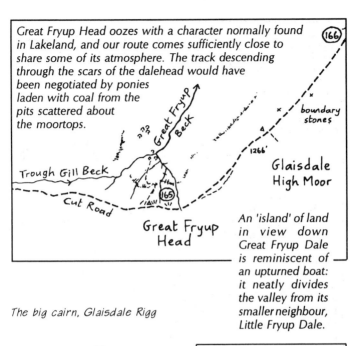

Great Fryup Head oozes with a character normally found in Lakeland, and our route comes sufficiently close to share some of its atmosphere. The track descending through the scars of the dalehead would have been negotiated by ponies laden with coal from the pits scattered about the moortops.

(166)

Great Fryup Beck

boundary stones

Trough Gill Beck

Cut Road

1266'

(165)

Great Fryup Head

Glaisdale High Moor

An 'island' of land in view down Great Fryup Dale is reminiscent of an upturned boat: it neatly divides the valley from its smaller neighbour, Little Fryup Dale.

The big cairn, Glaisdale Rigg

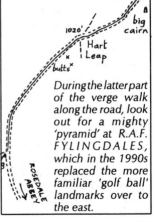

(167)

big cairn

1020'

Hart Leap

butts

ROSEDALE ABBEY

During the latter part of the verge walk along the road, look out for a mighty 'pyramid' at R.A.F. FYLINGDALES, which in the 1990s replaced the more familiar 'golf ball' landmarks over to the east.

125

This is the old road along Glaisdale Rigg, and is followed unerringly all the way down to its village, a super promenade regardless of the time and one's condition. Heather moor gives way to grass moor as height is lost, with the Eskdale scene increasing in clarity correspondingly. Eventually the old road meets a surfaced lanehead to drop down onto the green at the head of Glaisdale village.

There are several permutations of route from here to the railway station at the village foot, and these may depend upon the location of one's chosen lodging, if any. All steps first turn right, the direct route adhering to the main road that swings gracefully down to the station at Beggar's Bridge. Alternatively turn down a snicket above the terrace containing the Post office, and at the bottom follow a quieter back road along the dale floor; or stay on the road as far as the *Mitre Tavern*, and then strike left down a narrow road. All lead to the neighbourhood of Beggar's Bridge.

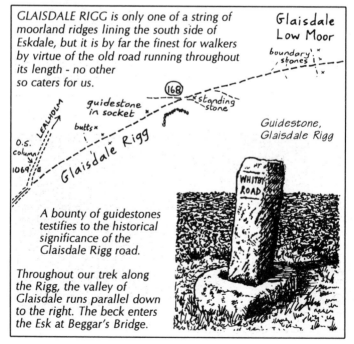

GLAISDALE RIGG is only one of a string of moorland ridges lining the south side of Eskdale, but it is by far the finest for walkers by virtue of the old road running throughout its length - no other so caters for us.

Glaisdale Low Moor

boundary stones

168

guidestone in socket

standing stone

LEALHOLM

butts

O.S. column

1069

Glaisdale Rigg

Guidestone, Glaisdale Rigg

WHITBY ROAD

A bounty of guidestones testifies to the historical significance of the Glaisdale Rigg road.

Throughout our trek along the Rigg, the valley of Glaisdale runs parallel down to the right. The beck enters the Esk at Beggar's Bridge.

GLAISDALE is a scattered village comprising of three distinct corners spreading from the environs of Beggar's Bridge up to the very edge of breezy Glaisdale Rigg. At the foot of its substantial side-valley, it boasts both lovely woods and rolling moors on its doorstep, and typifies the Esk Valley in its commendable attempts to deter the motor car from making logical progress: truly the railway is a necessity here. Peaceful today, Glaisdale was caught up in the 19th century iron ore 'boom' - when mining was in full swing one of its three hostelries underwent a name change to the 'Three Blast Furnaces', which were operating nearby. It still boasts three pubs and a tearoom to help slake your thirsts.

LEALHOLM

Esk Valley Line

River Esk

inn

Glaisdale Hall Farm

170

GLAISDALE HEAD

Glaisdale

inn

inn

169

This prominent embankment belongs to a long departed tramway to a former ironstone mine.

Beggar's Bridge, Glaisdale

127

GLAISDALE TO **ROBIN HOOD'S BAY**

20 miles   *1700 feet of ascent*

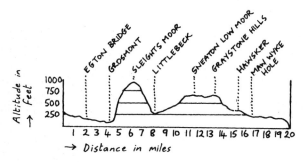

This final stage is an extravaganza of variety, comprising old toll road, steam trains, burial mounds, several tracts of heather moor, an idyllic hamlet, a beautiful waterfall in glorious woodland, and last but not least, an exhilarating clifftop. The only snag with this glorious finale is its length: by now you'll either be struggling gamely on to the end, or in condition to face up to Everest. If the former, then the prospect of crawling into Robin Hood's Bay as the sun sets, in no condition to undertake the ritual celebrations, will be sufficient to wish you'd planned a shorter last lap. This is best achieved by starting from Grosmont.

The wayward lurching of the route, however, is such that if you've bitten off too much, there are opportunities to omit sections - though little deserves missing. Anyway, here are the options. Take an old pannier way from Grosmont along the valley side to Sleights, and either cling to the valley floor to taste salt-water at Whitby, or cross from Sleights to Sneaton and pick up the route at Hawsker. Two easier finishes are a direct march from Graystone Hills; or a brisk walk along the old railway instead of the clifftop (this saves little). In totally different vein, consider heading north from Glaisdale to pick an interesting route to a finish at Staithes, similarly appointed to Robin Hood's Bay but less crowded.

At the railway station, Beggar's Bridge is hidden behind the long, low railway viaduct: pass under it to view the old pack bridge and then return to leave the road immediately by a footbridge over Glaisdale Beck to enter East Arnecliff Wood. The path climbs steeply, nears the river, and soon climbs again on a prolonged paved section. A gentler conclusion leads out onto a quiet road: turn down the hill towards Egton Bridge.

Pannier-way, East Arnecliff Wood

BEGGAR'S BRIDGE is a work of art, a graceful arched structure high above the Esk. The present bridge dates from the early 1600s, and served the packhorse era. It is said to have originally been built by Tom Ferris, a local lad who became the Mayor of Hull. Now a tourist attraction, it is sat incongruously between a dark railway bridge and a modern, featureless road bridge.

The path through EAST ARNECLIFF WOOD traces the course of a centuries-old pannier-way, one of many such trade routes that criss-cross Eskdale. Though packhorse days may be long gone, they still serve modern travellers.

First encountered at Beggar's Bridge, and sharing a similar valley-bottom course to us as far as Grosmont, is the ESK VALLEY LINE. A miracle survivor of Beeching's axe, this railway bears the hallmark of a rural line of several decades past. More importantly, the Middlesbrough-Whitby railway is a lifeline to the communities along its route, for the valley does not readily take to buses. Chasing the Esk through the winding dale floor, it bridges the river on no less than 18 occasions.

There is a tearoom on the station at Glaisdale.

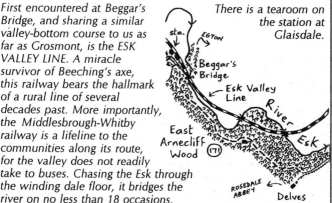

At a T-junction just past the *Horseshoe Inn* the way keeps on to the road bridge over the Esk, but a more attractive option is to go down some steps to the river, where dependable stepping stones cross it. Up onto the road, turn right to a junction between the church and the road bridge (Egton Bridge itself).

Depart Egton Bridge by the enclosed way almost opposite, signposted 'Egton Estates - private road'. Early on be sure to glance back to see Egton Manor, noting the ha-ha which keeps animals off the lawn without jarring the view. This former toll road runs along the valley floor of the Esk - passing a surviving notice of tolls - to emerge onto a road on the edge of Grosmont.

Turn right over the sturdy bridge to enter the village, along to the level crossing in the centre. Departure is simply by going straight on up the street climbing out, ignoring two branches left (both for Whitby via Sleights).

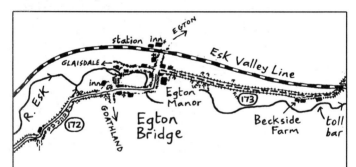

EGTON BRIDGE is a fascinating place for its size, rich in historical, natural and cultural attractions. Neighbour of the hilltop Egton village, it stands embowered in greenery in a particularly lovely corner of Eskdale. This was the birthplace of Nicholas Postgate, 'martyr of the moors'. After training in France he spent many post-Reformation decades working in this strongly Catholic district. Finally apprehended in 1679, he was hung, drawn and quartered for his 'crimes', on the Knavesmire at York, an old priest of 82. His memory is perpetuated by a village inn, and his faith by the beautiful church of St. Hedda, built in 1866 and famed for its detailed bas-relief panels set into the exterior walls, depicting scenes from the life of Christ.

GROSMONT is a pleasant village, firmly embedded at the foot of numerous steep roads. Dominated in the 19th century by ironstone mining (of which scars remain) there is less to see of earlier times, when - then as Grosmond - it supported an abbey of the little known Grantimontine order. Dissolved in 1536, Priory Farm occupies the site. Earlier still, a Roman fort existed in the neighbourhood. Today railways take centre stage, for here the Esk Valley Line meets the privately operated North Yorkshire Moors Railway, each with its own station. The Whitby-Pickering Railway opened in 1836 as a horse-drawn tramway, and a decade later was improved to take locomotives. The section south of Grosmont closed in 1965, only to be saved by enthusiasts and re-opened (initially to Goathland) in 1973. Today visitors can enjoy a steam-hauled 18 miles run to Pickering through the very heart of the moors - a memorable trip.

Grosmont (pronounced 'Grow-mont' - as in Bill Beaumont) has tearooms as well as its pub, the Station Inn.

The Murk Esk is largest of the Esk's many tributaries.

Further interest at Egton Bridge is found in its annual Gooseberry Show, held every August for two centuries. The toll road is another tradition - though the charges affixed to the cottage no longer apply.

Always, at Egton Bridge, there is of course the Esk itself, a famous salmon river and the National Park's major watercourse. Its journey from the moors to Whitby is one worth the following.

Surviving notice on the old toll road

BARNARD'S ROAD TOLL			
1 HORSE	2	WHEELS	4ᵈ
2 "	"	"	8ᵈ
1 "	4	"	8ᵇ
2 "	"	"	1ᶜ
3 "	"	"	1ᶜ
MOTOR CAR	4	"	1ᶜ
"	3	"	1ᶜ
MOTOR CYCLE SIDE CAR			1ᶜ
MOTOR LORRY			2ᶜ
MOTOR BUS			3ᶜ
TRACTOR			1ᶜ
HEARSE			6ᵇ
THIS GATE IS CLOSED AND LOCKED AT 10 PM DAILY			
EGTON ESTATES OFFICE AUG 1948			

The bridge, Grosmont

Though extensively damaged, the Bride Stones were originally circles at least 30 feet in diameter. FLAT HOWE is a round barrow in a kerb of retaining stones - heather enthusiastically covers it. Arousing greater enthusiasm for us, however, as we cross Sleights Moor, is the wide sweep of coastline in view. Whitby is revealed in near-entirety: it's a long time since we were near anywhere that size. Coincidentally enough, its relationship with Robin Hood's Bay is not dissimilar to that between Whitehaven and St Bees. Remember St Bees?

*Alternative route (see opposite): Initially unclear, it slants up towards the brow, then swings left, contouring round to improve into a good, clear path.

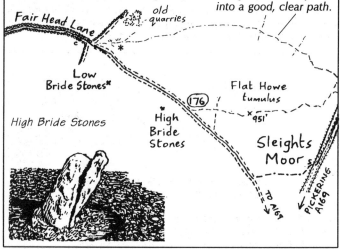

Fair Head Lane is a right old pull enlivened by the retrospective views over Eskdale to the moors above, and more significantly, a good seascape where Whitby Abbey claims prominence on its clifftop site. When the road breaks onto the open moor things start to relent (an off-road alternative route is shown on the map opposite). As the road heads on, the line of standing stones known as Low Bride Stones is seen skulking in a reedy patch of ground. Virtually level now, the road leads on past the more open aspect of High Bride Stones: these are fewer but more conspicuous.

The original route linked the stones with the distinct mound of Flat Howe on the crest of Sleights Moor, but as these non rights of way are frowned upon, continue along the road, and at a parking area on the right, guideposts send footpaths both ways. Go left on a thin trod through the heather, quickly crossing to a fence just short of the A169. Go left with it to a stile giving access to the road. Cross and go left on the broad verge towards the top of Blue Bank. After five minutes another stile sends a bridlepath right, down the moor, leaving heather for bracken. At the bottom a stony track is joined for the final yards to the head of a surfaced lane. Continue down, joining a through road to maintain this direct descent into the sylvan setting of the hamlet of Littlebeck.

Over either footbridge or ford climb the road as far as the second bend, where a kissing-gate on the right leads into the woods. A good path heads upstream, becoming temporarily diverted from Little Beck by a waterfall on a small tributary.

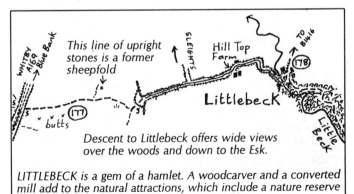

This line of upright stones is a former sheepfold

WHITBY A169 Blue Bank

SLEIGHTS

Hill Top Farm

TO B1416

178

Littlebeck

Little Beck

177 butts

Descent to Littlebeck offers wide views over the woods and down to the Esk.

LITTLEBECK is a gem of a hamlet. A woodcarver and a converted mill add to the natural attractions, which include a nature reserve in Littlebeck Wood. This is a little corner of heaven.

133

Falling Foss

Beyond a spoil heap continue on before climbing steeply to the Hermitage. Leave by the upper path, and when this quickly forks take the right branch, slanting down by a wall before running on to a fork. Keep right to descend to Falling Foss, arriving at a viewpoint above the falls. From the nearby footbridge, cross a farm road and head upstream. Within a minute the path fords the beck to lead upstream to the bridge at May Beck car park.

Turn up the road doubling back left, until just past the sharp bend above New May Beck Farm. A stony track strikes off over Sneaton Low Moor, quickly turning left and equally quickly becoming a narrower path through heather. Ahead, the B1416 is heard and then seen, long before it is joined. Turning right, a well-tramped verge provides pleasanter progress along this well-used road.

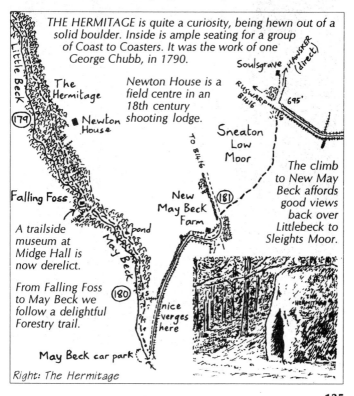

THE HERMITAGE is quite a curiosity, being hewn out of a solid boulder. Inside is ample seating for a group of Coast to Coasters. It was the work of one George Chubb, in 1790.

Little Beck

The Hermitage

Newton House

179

Soulsgrave

HAWSKER (direct)

Newton House is a field centre in an 18th century shooting lodge.

RUSWARP B1416

695'

Sneaton Low Moor

to B1416

New May Beck Farm

181

Falling Foss

pond

May Beck

A trailside museum at Midge Hall is now derelict.

From Falling Foss to May Beck we follow a delightful Forestry trail.

180

nice verges here

The climb to New May Beck affords good views back over Littlebeck to Sleights Moor.

May Beck car park

Right: The Hermitage

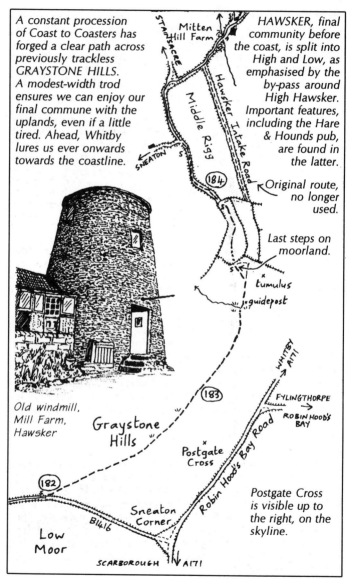

A constant procession of Coast to Coasters has forged a clear path across previously trackless GRAYSTONE HILLS. A modest-width trod ensures we can enjoy our final commune with the uplands, even if a little tired. Ahead, Whitby lures us ever onwards towards the coastline.

HAWSKER, final community before the coast, is split into High and Low, as emphasised by the by-pass around High Hawsker. Important features, including the Hare & Hounds pub, are found in the latter.

STAINSACRE

Mitten Hill Farm

Middle Rigg

Hawsker Intake Road

(184)

SNEATON

←Original route, no longer used.

Last steps on moorland.

× tumulus

∙guidepost

Old windmill, Mill Farm, Hawsker

Graystone Hills

(183)

(182)

Low Moor

B1416

Sneaton Corner

SCARBOROUGH

Postgate Cross ×

Robin Hood's Bay Road

WHITBY A171

FYLINGTHORPE →

ROBIN HOOD'S BAY

Postgate Cross is visible up to the right, on the skyline.

A171

136

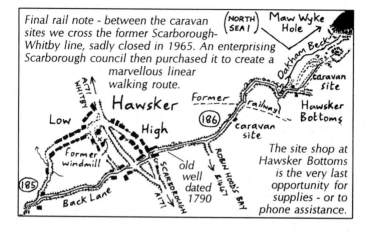

Final rail note - between the caravan sites we cross the former Scarborough-Whitby line, sadly closed in 1965. An enterprising Scarborough council then purchased it to create a marvellous linear walking route.

(NORTH SEA!)

Maw Wyke Hole

Oakham Beck

caravan site

Hawsker Bottoms

Hawsker

Former Railway

Low

High

186

caravan site

A171 WHITBY

former windmill

185

SCARBOROUGH A171

old well dated 1790

ROBIN HOOD'S BAY

Back Lane

The site shop at Hawsker Bottoms is the very last opportunity for supplies - or to phone assistance.

Before too long a stile on the other side of the road gives access to the great heathery tracts of Graystone Hills. With a seascape ahead again, another clear path heads away for a magic stroll away from the busy A171 over to the right. Happily this road is avoided as the path swings further north to cling tenaciously to a final march of heather. With the culmination of moorland walking just ahead, a guidepost beyond a small marsh sends the walk bearing left off the old path, to locate a stile in the fence. Head away, a path soon forming in an area of rampant gorse. The red roofs of Hawsker appear and the way drops between the bushes to a stile in the bottom left corner. Now enclosed by exuberant hedgerows, a slim path descends to emerge onto the sharp bend of a back road. Continue downhill, then at a junction turn right for Hawsker. The A171 is a final obstacle before entering the village street.

Continue out along the road to Robin Hood's Bay, and when it swings right keep straight on, past one caravan site and down to a second one. Just past the site shop the road ends, and here descend the site road through the caravans, continuing down as a path takes over to meet the coast path above Maw Wyke Hole, and thus, after a long absence, the Cleveland Way. This is indeed a classic moment: reaching the coast is sufficiently thrilling, but the grandeur of the scenery makes it doubly satisfying. Turn right to savour the final miles.

The way ahead is distinctly obvious as it is bounded on one side by majestic cliffs and thence the North Sea. On eventually rounding Ness Point beneath a coastguard lookout, Robin Hood's Bay comes fully into view, and the village itself is soon within our sights. At last a kissing-gate leads into trees to emerge onto a residential street, Mount Pleasant North. At the end turn left to descend the bustling main street all the way down through the heart of the village to its inevitable conclusion. Keep on out onto the stony shore, just as far as the North Sea happens to be, and that's it, you've done it!

ROBIN HOOD'S BAY, with the advantages of an exciting name and an even better location, will be found on many people's list of favourite places. Once the quiet preserve of fishermen and smugglers, it is now very much part of the tourist itinerary. Known in the locality simply as Bay Town, it consists of a chaotic tumble of red-roofed buildings squeezed into a narrow break in the cliffs. From the modern extension on the clifftop, the steep main street plunges down to the very sea. On each side are irregular groupings of shops and dwellings, with narrow passageways linking the near-hidden doorsteps. It also boasts four public houses in which to celebrate!

Over the years the village has suffered greatly from storms, and the savage waters once drove a ship into the Bay Hotel: a modern seawall now ensures rather more safety. The bay itself is regarded as a geologists' mecca, with fossils and eager school parties in equal abundance.

Boggle Hole Youth Hostel

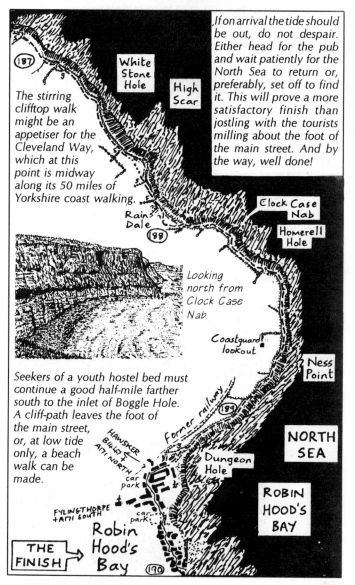

(187)

White Stone Hole

High Scar

The stirring clifftop walk might be an appetiser for the Cleveland Way, which at this point is midway along its 50 miles of Yorkshire coast walking.

If on arrival the tide should be out, do not despair. Either head for the pub and wait patiently for the North Sea to return or, preferably, set off to find it. This will prove a more satisfactory finish than jostling with the tourists milling about the foot of the main street. And by the way, well done!

Rains Dale

(188)

Clock Case Nab

Homerell Hole

Looking north from Clock Case Nab

Coastguard lookout

Ness Point

Seekers of a youth hostel bed must continue a good half-mile farther south to the inlet of Boggle Hole. A cliff-path leaves the foot of the main street, or, at low tide only, a beach walk can be made.

Former railway

(189)

HAWSKER
BILLET +
A171 NORTH

car park

NORTH SEA

Dungeon Hole

ROBIN HOOD'S BAY

FYLINGTHORPE
+A171 SOUTH

car park

Robin Hood's Bay

THE FINISH ➜

(190)

RECORD OF THE JOURNEY

Date	Place	Miles		Notes
		daily	total	
	St Bees	-	-	
	Sandwith	4½	4½	
	Cleator	8½	8½	
	Dent	10½	10½	
	Ennerdale Bridge	14	14	
	Gillerthwaite	5	19	
	Black Sail Hut	9	23	
	Honister Pass	11½	25½	
	Seatoller	13¼	27¼	
	Rosthwaite	14½	28½	
	Stonethwaite	1	29½	
	Greenup Edge	3¾	32¼	
	Easedale	8	36½	
	Grasmere	9	37½	
	Grisedale Hause	12½	41	
	Patterdale	17½	46	
	Boredale Hause	1	47	
	Kidsty Pike	5	51	
	Haweswater	6¾	52¾	
	Burnbanks	11	57	
	Rosgill Bridge	13	59	
	Shap	16	62	
	Oddendale	3	65	
	Orton	8¼	70¼	
	Sunbiggin Tarn	12¾	74¾	
	Smardale Bridge	17	79	
	Waitby junction	19	81	
	Kirkby Stephen	21	83	
	Hartley	1	84	
	9 Standards Rigg	5¼	88¼	
	Raven Seat	9¼	92¼	
	Keld	12	95	

RECORD OF THE JOURNEY

Date	Place	Miles daily	total	Notes
	Gunnerside Gill	3½	98½	
	Surrender Bridge	7½	102½	
	Reeth	11	106	
	Grinton	1¼	107¼	
	Marrick	3¾	109¾	
	Marske	6¼	112¼	
	Richmond	11	117	
	Colburn	3	120	
	Catterick Bridge	5¾	122¾	
	Bolton on Swale	7½	124½	
	Danby Wiske	14	131	
	Oaktree Hill	16	133	
	Long Lane	18½	135½	
	A19	22	139	
	Ingleby Cross	23	140	
	Beacon Hill	2	142	
	Huthwaite Green	5	145	
	Carlton Bank	8	148	
	The Wainstones	10¾	150¾	
	Clay Bank Top	12	152	
	Round Hill	1¾	153¾	
	Bloworth Crossing	3¼	155¼	
	Lion, Blakey	8¾	160¾	
	Trough House	12	164	
	Glaisdale	18	170	
	Beggar's Bridge	½	170½	
	Egton Bridge	2½	172½	
	Grosmont	4½	174½	
	Littlebeck	8	178	
	New May Beck	11	181	
	Hawsker	15½	185½	
	Robin Hood's Bay	20	190	

RECORD OF ACCOMMODATION

Date	Address	Notes

RECORD OF PUBS VISITED

Name	Location	Notes

INDEX

Place names on the route maps

144

INDEX continued

THE FELLOWSHIP OF THE COAST TO COAST

These pages are reserved as a special memento of the walk, perhaps for autographs & addresses of friends made along the way. Even the most hermit-like of walkers are bound to encounter like-minded souls, and a suitable reminder of happy events makes a nice personal touch. If you do manage to avoid human contact, then use the space for important notes such as the time of your train home!

Looking down into the head of Farndale

East Gill Force, Keld

Honister Crag